AF489710

# TO END A WAR

A Short History of Human Rights,
the Rule of Law, and How
Drug Prohibition Violates
the Bill of Rights

Roar Mikalsen

# TO THE YOUTH
## WHO ALWAYS OUTRUN
## FAKE AUTHORITY

# CONTENTS:

# 1

# The Rule of Law*

*"Since no man has a natural authority over his fellow, and force creates no right, we must conclude that conventions form the basis of all legitimate authority among men."*

—*Jean-Jacques Rousseau, 1762*—

OUR GOVERNMENTS ARE proud defenders of a freedom-loving tradition that can be traced back to the French Revolution and the American Declaration of Independence. In the late 1700s, these events led to the establishment of important ruling principles. Until this time, nations were ruled by all-powerful kings. These kings claimed that their authority was given from God and below them were the nobles, the knights, and the clergy. The individuals in these groups had certain privileges, varying according to their wealth and power, and under them were ordinary people, having no rights at all. Society was a

---

* This treatise provides a general idea of the issues discussed. The endnotes go a long way in documenting assertions and for a better understanding, see ROAR MIKALSEN, *TO RIGHT A WRONG: A CONSTITUTIONAL FRAMEWORK FOR CONSTITUTIONAL CONSTRUCTION* (2016) or ROAR MIKALSEN, *HUMAN RISING: THE PROHIBITIONIST PSYCHOSIS AND ITS CONSTITUTIONAL IMPLICATIONS* (2018).

strict, hierarchical structure, and most people depended on the mercy of their superior.

In the late 1700s, however, this system was in for a change. It was an exciting time in Western history. Today, we remember it as the Age of Reason (or the Enlightenment Era), and as people wised up, the pressure for reform was building. People would no longer accept the strict class distinctions. They were fed up with centuries of increasing exploitation and oppression and sought to end their disenfranchised societal status. They therefore demanded a certain modicum of dignity and control over their lives, and the result was the emergence of human rights, as well as other governing doctrines. These doctrines had a foundation in principled thinking. At the heart of our constitutional heritage, the values, ideals, and principles connected to wholeness were the basis of contractual thinking, and equality, proportionality, autonomy, popular sovereignty, separation of powers, and a liberty presumption were set to guide us.

Today, every government with respect for itself (and its people) recognizes these principles and has incorporated them into its Constitution. The principle of popular sovereignty states that all power emanates from the people. This means that the State itself has no rights, it is just an organizational body created to assist the people. The State's employees are therefore public servants and, as the title holds, their sole duty and responsibility is to serve the people. Consequently, the State has no rights as seen in relation to the individuals, and people, in turn, have no obligations towards the State. Their only obligation is to follow its laws and regulations, which in turn draw their legitimacy from the people, but—and this is important—*only insofar as these laws and regulations are in line with the human rights conventions.*

These conventions define the boundaries for the State's rightful exercise of power, and they are the result of a historical lesson that we would do well to remember. This lesson is that those who govern tend to adopt laws that are not necessarily in the interest of the public. This may be laws which are put in place to gratify the ruling elite's urge for social, political, or economic control. Legislation directed towards religious or ethnic minority groups, laws that prohibit homosexuality, as well as other discriminatory practices, are examples. Such laws have no inherent legitimacy as they violate overriding principles, and many great thinkers have pointed this out. Aristotle, for instance, said 2500 years ago that "even when laws have been written down, they ought not always to remain unaltered." Thomas Aquinas said 800 years ago that "Human law is law only by virtue of its accordance with right reason, and by this means it is clear that it flows from Eternal Law. In so far as it deviates from right reason it is called an unjust law; and in such a case it is no law at all, but rather an assertion of violence." Charles Montesquieu remarked 250 years ago that "there is no crueller tyranny than that which is perpetuated under the shield of law and in the name of justice," and another bright man, Albert Camus, stated in the 1950s that "the law's final justification is the good it does or fails to do in the society of a given place and time."

At any given time, then, there have been both just and unjust laws. To put it simply, *just laws* are those laws which are compatible with the ideals, values, and principles that connect to wholeness. These laws ensure a social dynamic that is beneficial for individuals and society alike, while *unjust laws* are those that inflict a more unfortunate dynamic. They build from totalitarian premises and they tie us down and limit our potential instead of protecting us against injustice.

It is not always easy to know what type of law we are dealing with. No matter how inhumane, there will be people who believe that a law is necessary (that without it everything would have been worse), and no matter how useful the law, there will be some who find it objectionable. History is full of examples of legislation which, at one point, were accepted as necessary and legitimate, but that later generations found reprehensible and did away with.

That laws have an expiration date may be construed as a paradox. As we shall see, the legal principles upon which our laws are based are both simple and eternal, and so one should think that a nation's laws reflected this fact. This, however, is not the case, and the reason is that we are born into a world where the moral climate is so powerful that it blinds us to these principles' eternal light. In fact, it takes a rare effort to connect with this light, as the delusional waters of our culture muddy our mind and make principled perspective difficult.

Nonetheless, there have always been people with access to this timeless world of ideas. This will be that percentage of the population who has advanced cognitively to the point where they have left behind the bewildering mists of the collective psyche. They are therefore able to see their age in a historical context and, thanks to their commitment, the light of these principles is slowly transforming the social fabric, bringing us closer to Utopia.

In other words, it is as a result of our increasing wisdom that Eternal Law becomes manifest. I say, "Eternal Law" because these ideas are derived from the wholeness and as civilizations evolve, they become more and more inspired by those values, norms, and ideals that mirror its oneness. As society matures, we understand that these ideals taken seriously have the power to help us out of our misery, and so people see them as a roadmap that, if followed, will help us reclaim our inherent greatness.

This is what we all intuitively recognize. Only those with an agenda of their own or those ignorant of Eternal Law will object and so, as humanity has evolved, we see how the laws of the land have aligned with these principles. Today, a majority believe that we have advanced to the point where disproportional, arbitrary, and discriminatory practices are evils of the past. Yet, nothing does more damage to a society than unjust laws, and, wise from injury, we know that later generations may see things differently.

These are the understandings that have brought about our legal framework. And if our public servants want to ban some activity, therefore, before they pass a law, they must ensure that it is in accordance with the provisions of human rights conventions. These conventions represent the epitome of the maturation process mentioned above. They are the firmament that anchor the vision of Higher law, and since the end of the

18<sup>th</sup> century, when their principles were formally recognized, their societal priority and position has become increasingly important. Today, they stand above all other laws, and if the State wants to be a legitimate entity, it must protect the rights of citizens as articulated in the human rights conventions. To the extent that the State fails in this quest, it is no longer governed by the rule of law—and if it is no longer a rule of law, it is a police state.

Throughout history, we find that special interest groups have been eager to pursue power and privilege. It is the rule that power is never evenly distributed, and those who have a lot have used their wealth to influence the political process. Historically, the chief means of advancing elites have been blackmailing, bribery, and extortion. The Epstein scandal is just a recent reminder of the greater game that is being played, and it is for this reason that the constitution recognizes the problem and aims at keeping in check would-be usurpers. If there is not, there will be a social dynamic where the distance between those who govern and those who are governed increases, until it becomes obvious that the State is no longer a representative of the people but rather has become a tool of the ruling class, used to keep the population under control.

History speaks volumes about this, and so we have a legal framework which recognizes the problem and means to ensure that rights are protected. This framework is the human rights apparatus[*] and its purpose is to protect against unreasonable

---

[*] When it comes to protection of rights, two systems have emerged: The Global/European model and the American. This book speaks to the former,

and arbitrary interference by the government. To Europeans, our human rights are protected by the European Convention of Human Rights, the UN Charter and human rights conventions, and the constitution of each member state. This framework speaks to the requirements that any legislation must meet to be legitimate: It guarantees a fair trial—and if a defendant argues that his natural rights have been violated, he shall have an effective remedy.

This means that if a Christian (or Muslim, Hindu, etc.) lives in a place that has forbidden religion, he is free to violate the law and practice religion. Then, if arrested for doing so, he can use his rights to challenge the law. Every signatory to the human rights apparatus has outlawed arbitrary, discriminatory, and disproportional laws, and so, if a citizen tells the judge that a law is in violation of human rights, the magistrate is obligated to let the issue be determined by an independent, impartial, and competent court. The defendant must document why he is the victim of a discriminatory, disproportional, and arbitrary practice. But if the Court finds that a defendant is right, everyone is free to practice religion and the law must be changed.

It is not often that citizens make use of the right to a fair trial and demand a judicial review on human rights grounds. Few are even aware that they have this right, but it is a key aspect of the rule of law and a result of principles such as popular sovereignty and separation of powers. We have seen the first mean that a law shall reflect the power of the people

---

while the latter is explained in MIKALSEN, *CONSTITUTIONAL CHALLENGES TO THE DRUG LAW: A CASE STUDY* (2017)

and not the government, and the second principle emphasizes the independence of the courts.

As mentioned, it is because the political process is at risk of being overtaken by self-serving elites that we have a society built on these principles. There is also a danger of society succumbing to moral panic and destructive mass movements. History speaks volumes, and the principles of law are there to set the record straight. According to the separation of powers, therefore, government must be separated into three branches: the legislative, executive, and judiciary. This separation of powers is a safety valve built into the system, and the three branches shall control each other to make sure that tyrannical government does not arise.

An independent press adds to this, as it is intended to provide additional insurance that special interest groups do not become too powerful. However, there remains a possibility that certain groups, through blackmail, violence, or bribery, can become so influential that the political process fails. There is also the danger of a tyranny by majority rule, and there is no shortage of societies where the scapegoating phenomenon has been sufficiently powerful to overcome the rule of law. This mechanism, which arises from ineptitude and self-deception on part of the individual to inspire mass movements of arbitrary persecution in the collective, has been the great problem of human rights. Since the building of societies, the tendency to blame others for problems that are a collective responsibility has been the engine of human rights violations across the globe, and we need not look further than the drug law to find an example. As we shall see, it has been well known for several decades that drug prohibition results from misconceptions and false premises; that it was brought into being by a corrupt political process; that prohibitionists abused or ignored the available evidence; and that voices of reason were subdued or ignored.[1] While prohibitionists will disagree, the evidence is overwhelming. To this day, no knowledgeable professional has endorsed prohibition, and this is hardly controversial. Professors of criminology and sociology John F. Galliher, David P. Keys, and Michael Elsner elaborates:

*"Since the 1960s, few criminologists or criminal law professors have supported government drug policies. To this day, those setting . . . drug policy continue to ignore expert legal, academic, and medical advice. In the academic community there is now a clear recognition of long-standing patterns of both the ineffectiveness of, and racism inherent in . . . drug law enforcement. Indeed, opposition to contemporary . . . drug control policy has become normative in the academic community."[2]*

As a matter of fact, the drug law has survived to this day supported by nothing but the empty rhetoric of self-serving bureaucrats,[3] and there is evidence that a regime of regulation would be a more sensible solution.[4] It is also easy to demonstrate that public officials should have taken this evidence into consideration long ago. As Kofi Annan, former UN Secretary General, and Louise Arbour, former UN High Commissioner for Human Rights, commented:

*"It might have been understandable that the architects of the system would place faith in the concept of eradicating drug production and use (in the light of the limited evidence available at the time). There is no excuse, however, for ignoring the evidence and experience accumulated since then. . . . There is a temptation to avoid the issue. This is an abdication of policy responsibility—for every year we continue with the current approach, billions of dollars are wasted on ineffective programs, millions of citizens are sent to prison unnecessarily, millions more suffer from the drug dependence of loved ones who cannot access health and social care services, and hundreds of thousands of people die from preventable overdoses and diseases contracted through unsafe drug use."*[5]

Again, prohibitionists may disagree, but proof is everywhere to be found. An Australian expert group, for instance, concluded in 2012 that "By maintaining prohibition and suppressing or avoiding debate about its costs and benefits, it can be argued justifiably that our governments and other community leaders are standing idly by while our children are killed and criminalized."[6] Moreover, a European panel of experts concluded thus after reviewing the status quo:

*"Despite the primacy of human rights obligations under the UN Charter, the approach of the UN system and the international community to addressing the tensions*

*between drug control and human rights remains marked by an ambiguity that is inexcusable in the face of the egregious human rights abuses perpetrated in the course of enforcing drug prohibition. . . . It is past time for UN, its individual Members, and its organs, as well as civil society organizations, to ensure that the international drug control system works to respect, protect and fulfill the human rights of people who use drugs and affected communities, and to hold the international drug control entities and UN Members to account for human rights abuses committed in the name of drug control.*"[7]

This was more than a decade ago. Since then, many more billions of dollars have been wasted on counterproductive policies, more than 20 million people have been wrongfully imprisoned, and another million, at least, have died as a direct consequence of the war on drugs.[8]

For some reason, however, our leaders have failed to recognize the critique against drug prohibition, and they have learned nothing from the past 50 years. This is important because, if we can prove that the drug laws are an arbitrary, discriminatory, and disproportional practice—and if we confront them with this evidence—politicians are obligated to take this evidence into consideration and to check if it is so. It is also important because, if the political process has become corrupted and the state apparatus is no longer able to control the quality of the law, citizens can go to the judiciary to check if the law is in violation of their rights.

The human rights conventions are clear, and the relation between the drug laws and the human rights law shall be elaborated on. Before we go on, however, let us summarize the reasoning that underpins our legal order:

> *To begin with, the individual is the alpha and omega:* We are all born free and equal; we all have the same inherent right to pursue our happiness; and we all have the same right to self-determination over our lives and our property—be it our body, our thoughts, or our possessions.

> *This is the fundamental premise from which everything follows.* However, we also know that individuals do not always behave towards their fellowmen. Some people forcibly intervene in the lives of others, and so we have created the State, with its monopoly of force, to safeguard individual rights, provide safe and supportive communities, and to ensure that the social machinery functions optimally.

> *This is the social contract.* The state apparatus, however, can never be better than the quality of the collective consciousness. And as mankind is a rather immature entity consisting of individuals who all too often see self-interest and public interest as mutually exclusive, the state apparatus, as a result of us living in a class-divided society, has become a playground for

special interests seeking to advance their own agendas rather than the public interest.

➢ *This is the fundamental problem facing humanity.* To ensure a balance of power, therefore, we have a separation of powers and with an independent press to keep an eye on everything, we have a firmament which is to ensure that no single group takes control of the state apparatus.

➢ Still, there remains a chance that special interest groups can overcome these safety measures. And to limit the possibility that the State becomes a tool for the ruling class' oppression of the majority, we have a legal framework where human rights law rules supreme.

➢ *This legal framework is available to all people.* The purpose of human rights law is to protect the inherent dignity of the individual by ensuring that the State does not unnecessarily and overbroadly interfere in our lives. It therefore establishes certain criteria with which all laws must comply, and it ensures an effective remedy against undue restrictions.

# 2

# The Problem with the State

*"No government is, or can be, committed to freedom. Only people can be. Government, by its very nature, has a vested interest in enlarging its freedom of action, thereby necessarily reducing the freedom of individuals."*[9]

*—Thomas Szasz, professor of psychiatry—*

BEFORE LOOKING AT the human rights conventions, we need to discuss the relationship between the individual and the State. The purpose of human rights law, after all, is to protect the individual from undue governmental intrusion, and for a good reason. History is clear that the greatest threat facing humanity has been its rulers: in the 20th century, between 200-300 million people died because of political ambitions, and looking back, a constant is the increasingly oppressive intervention of government in all areas of life.

Now, officials are not keen to admit this. However, the proof is in the pudding and the State's and the individual's sphere of influence must be seen as two opposing poles: To the extent that one is reinforced, the other will be reduced, and so we should see the State as a wolf in sheep's clothing.

This is not to say that all civil servants are psychopaths with an overriding ambition of despotism. Not at all. But despite good intentions, our officials are part of a larger body, and this body's primary concern is its own survival. People familiar with the workings of government can testify to this, and no matter how detrimental to society, organizations and agencies will justify their existence in the pursuit of bigger budgets and more powers.

Hence, the most significant characteristic of a bureaucracy is its tendency to feed itself. And looking back, we see how this dynamic has made the State become ever more powerful, reducing the individual's sphere of influence.

Again, it is not my intention to disparage public officials. But like I said, they are part of a greater organizational apparatus, and this greater apparatus wants to expand its influence, regardless of merits. This is important to recognize. After all, the bigger the government, the more enslaved a population, and so, while disciples of Government talk of "freedom" and "human rights" as if the fight for these ideals was truly spearheaded by government, intelligent minds will know that it cannot be so. They will understand that the State cannot possibly be a champion of freedom or civil rights because the State, by virtue of its very nature, has a vested interest in increasing its sphere of influence, which it can only do at the expense of ours.

In other words, *only individuals* can be freedom fighters and human rights defenders. We see time and time again how organizations fail us—and the bigger the organization, the more likely it is to be corrupted by systemic incentives. This is the only reason why "watchdogs" like Amnesty International, Human Rights Watch, etc., have accepted the status quo. In times of moral panic, which has been detected,[*] principled thinking is simply too controversial to influence policy and budgets and operations become problematic if taboos are not honored. Hence, the more principled, the more likely public officials are to be estranged from the herd—and that the State, despite insurances to the contrary, represents a threat is shown by history and current conditions. After all, if *freedom* is to have any meaning, it must be a measure of the power to do with our own lives and property as we please. *Only to the degree that this is actualized* will the right to life, liberty, and the pursuit of happiness have any meaning, and looking at it this way, we have never been more enslaved.

Drug prohibition is a case in point, as until the $20^{th}$ century people took as granted the right to self-medicate. If they were sick, their favorite medicines were opiates, cocaine, and cannabis derivatives, and they could not have imagined that later generations would see things so differently. Even so, here we are, and a majority now accepts that the State claims a

---

[*] For more on this phenomenon, see MIKALSEN, *HUMAN RISING* (2021). Moral panic has been noted by many reports and commissions, see for instance NOU 2019: 26, Rusreform – fra straff til hjelp (Drug Law Reform – from punishment to help). In its chapter 3, the Norwegian Royal Commission on Drug Policy use words such as "public panic", "unbalanced views", "misleading perceptions", "misapplication of punishment", and "reality-resistant iniquity" to summarize the development of drug policy. We are dealing with a debate characterized by "stereotypical representations", "moral indignation and revenge urges", one where "scientific understanding of the drug problem has played a minor role." "Panic" is used several times.

right to control the most intimate aspect of our lives—our own consciousness.

Our leaders hope that we do not notice or react to this ever-widening gap between theory and practice. The system is put together so that those who drift with systemic currents will get promoted, and so, generally speaking, the people at the top have divested of all integrity. They have effectively become system-zombies and will argue in favor of power.

Understanding this mechanism is of utmost importance. Human rights law, after all, is put together to protect the individual against unjust interference, and so, looking back, it should come as no surprise that the State has had an ambivalent relationship to the ideals and principles enshrined in our constitutions.

A quick 101-course reveals the reasons for this, as all governments trace their origin back to a band of robbers who joined forces to plunder, control, and subjugate the rest of the population. The formation of governments was the natural result of their ambition, and the making of laws their method for keeping the people in subjugation. Hence, the discipline of law originated in the desires of one class of persons to plunder and enslave others and to hold them as property.

For obvious reasons this is not taught in law school. No oppressor has ever given the oppressed the keys to their liberty and so the truth becomes taboo. Even so, speaking of human rights, we better understand the origins of government and the evolution of law. It was because of the threat from government that the system of Roman law gave way to a more evolved system of human rights. And as its purpose is (1) to protect the individual from arbitrary rule and (2) to secure an effective remedy against undue interference, it is the antithesis to the older system of law.

It is for this reason that the history of human rights has been a battle between those with a primary ambition to power and those who are guided by a more profound loyalty to humanity. Even if the servants of the status quo come and go, the old system of oppression remains intact to this day, and so there remains an interesting dynamic between those jurists who care about the connection between morality and law and those who do not.

While the former, historically, have been representatives of the natural law tradition, the latter group has been called positivists. The positivists focus on the law *as it is,* while the naturalists are concerned with the larger picture and imagine the law *as it should be.* They see justice as an ideal, not as the actions of authority, and their questioning of authority makes them difficult to rulers. This is why positivists have been embraced by governments, because they have no regard for morals. Nevertheless, it is the natural law tradition that has inspired our constitutional heritage. David Bergland, former presidential candidate for the United States Libertarian Party, explains the difference:

*"Under positivism, there logically cannot be, should not be, and are, no limits on government because it is the source of rights and the power to protect those rights. Why do I call it a fallacy? For the reason that acceptance of this view deprives us of any effective*

*defense of the ultimate political value: liberty for ourselves as individuals, while leaving the field open to all forms of dictatorship and slavery. Positivism leads to totalitarianism in practice because it recognizes no logical way to argue against any exercise of government power over the individual. It leads to draconian limits on freedom of speech, press or any kind of dissent, to mass murder of dissidents, and to economic and environmental disaster as demonstrated in Nazi Germany, the former Soviet Union and Eastern Europe.*

*The post-World War II War Crimes trials in Nuremberg illuminate the issue. The Nazi defendants claimed they were merely enforcing the law of the State, just following orders issued from the legitimate heads of the German State. That should be a valid defense in a purely positivist regime, but not one where natural rights views predominate. Indeed, the convictions at Nuremburg could only be sustained on the basis that the individual victims had rights superior to what the Nazi government recognized and that those rights had been violated by the defendants while carrying out the State orders to exterminate them.*

*The consequences of consistently applied positivism in practice are anti-liberty, anti-rights, anti-human and anti-life. Anyone who values liberty and the flourishing of individual human beings in conditions of peace and abundance must begin by rejecting the view that it is morally appropriate for government to act in every situation that displeases us.*"[10]

While Bergland notes important issues, there are also positivists who recognize that there are limits to the government's just intrusion. In fact, human rights law being acknowledged as the supreme law of the land, it is difficult even for a positivist not to accept its obligations. Even so, quite a few sticks with positivism to justify and legitimize transgressions on our catalogue of rights. Such jurists care not about the morality of law or their actions. Their ambition is more concerned with "practical affairs"—i.e., to serve the status quo and to make a living of other people's misery.

Looking at history, we find that, in defense against some perceived threat, these jurists have endorsed genocide, slavery, segregation, torture, drug laws, and more. And while the natural law jurists have had no other ambition than to build a supportive basis for Higher law, positivists cling on to totalitarian premises. Not always explicitly, as they may pay lip-service to the values, norms, ideals, and principles that others adhere to. Still, nothing is more threatening to agents of power than the standards and principles of human rights law. Principles of autonomy, equality, proportionality, non-arbitrariness, and a presumption of liberty have the power to expose oppression and deceit wherever it exists. They will illuminate any distance between theory and practice, and so authorities have sought to limit their influence. As a result, their light has never been allowed to truly shine, and agents of power have put great effort into maintaining a culture of impunity by controlling human rights institutions.

While never officially recognized, this mechanism is in effect today, just as it was 300 years ago. No matter where we look, bureaucracies are caught in a tug-of-war between those officials who unyieldingly seek to advance the progress of human rights law and those who are guided by more ignoble incentives. The former has sought an open, enlightened examination of the facts, one that allows for the truth, while the latter have opposed any such activity. Knowing intuitively, if not intellectually, that their position cannot be rationally defended, they have empowered an enemy image; they have relied on misdirection, cover-ups and outright lies to avoid unpleasant truths; they have let arrogance, prejudice, and ignorance inform their policies; they have encouraged fallacies and narrow-mindedness to promote self-serving agendas; and they have watered-down our catalogue of rights. Thus, they have kept the light of reason from interfering. But even though they may have represented the majority of our officials, others have had truth on their side.

Now truth, as the saying goes, lives a wretched life. Nevertheless, it always survives a lie, and as a result reform activists have gained ground. The history of human rights law is itself a testimony to this—and now that we know better than to trust authorities to protect our rights, we shall have a look at the Bill of Rights.

# 3

# The Bill of Rights
# and the Drug Law

*"Ignorance, neglect, or contempt of human rights, are the sole causes of public misfortunes and corruptions of Government."*

*—Declaration of the Rights of Man and Citizen, 1789—*

IT WAS ONLY after the atrocities of the Second World War, with the formation of the UN, that the issue of human rights was taken seriously by governments. The concept, however, is not new and our human rights conventions are the result of Enlightenment Era thinking. The French Declaration of the Rights of Man mirrored this. It was among the first of its kind[*] and as "ignorance, neglect, or contempt of human rights" was believed to be "the sole cause of public calamities and corruptions of government", its authors wrote a declaration to remind the government of its duties.

---

[*] The Virginia Declaration of Rights, the precursor to the American Bill of Rights, was written in 1776 and preceded it.

Thus, the purpose of the first human rights declaration was to establish "the natural, unalienable, and sacred rights of man". It set a standard that the State had to abide by and based upon incontestable principles, it formulated articles whereby grievances could be addressed.

The modern human rights apparatus elaborates on this thinking. The idea is that all people are born equal; that we share the right to life, liberty, and the pursuit of happiness (i.e., a right to develop character and our inherent potential), and that we all share the same rights and obligations. Furthermore, the State shall guarantee the protection of rights. As discussed, it shall serve the public/greater good and ensure that no group of privileged few infringes on the rights of others. It shall distribute benefits and obligations, and to the extent that freedom is limited, there must be compelling societal considerations. *Our laws, then, shall be a mutual protection against injustice.* And as Rawls's first principle of justice holds, each person is to have an equal right to the most extensive liberty compatible with a similar liberty for others.

In short, this is the essence of the social contract, and the State is a non-entity. It has no rights of its own: it is only a service apparatus constructed for the purpose of securing our rights and ensuring that the machinery of society functions optimally—and that is all. The slogan of the French Revolution "Liberty, Equality, and Fraternity" sums up the modern project and as a result, human rights conventions have come into being. While some conventions, like the European Convention of Human Rights, only apply to The European continent, citizens of the world are protected by the United

Nations' International Bill of Human Rights. This includes the Universal Declaration of Human Rights, as well as other conventions (or Covenants)[*], and when we discuss human rights, we refer to a set of standards outlined in this Bill; standards that define certain criteria that all laws must comply with.

Now, there are different articles in this Bill, and we shall become familiar with a few. These articles, however, are part of a greater picture. Human rights being indivisible, interrelated, and inter-dependent, they are built on principled thinking and their purpose is to protect against undue government intrusion.

As we just saw, the State has a tendency to expand its sphere of influence at the expense of ours. Human rights law recognizes this, and so it establishes a set of principles and norms intended to protect the individual against unlawful State actions. While these principles have names, such as autonomy, equality, proportionality, and non-arbitrariness, they are interrelated and interdependent. This means that if a law is discriminatory, it is also arbitrary, disproportional, and unjust, and it all depends on the test of reason. We shall now see how the drug laws are measured and found wanting when subjected to its analysis.

---

[*] In 1966, two International Covenants on Human Rights were completed. These were the International Covenant on Economic, Social and Cultural Rights (ICESCR) and the International Covenant on Civil and Political Rights (ICCPR), which effectively translated the principles of the Universal Declaration into treaty law. In conjunction with the Universal Declaration of Human Rights, the two Covenants are referred to as the International Bill of Human Rights.

# 3. 1. Drug Prohibition and Human Rights

*"As man develops, he places a greater value upon his own rights. Liberty becomes a grander and diviner thing. As he values his own rights, he begins to value the rights of others. And when all men give to all others all the rights they claim for themselves, this world will be civilized."*

*—Robert G. Ingersoll, lawyer—*

When it comes to drug laws and human rights, much can be said. In fact, drug prohibition is incompatible with principles of equality, fairness, proportionality, and justice as we have come to accept the application of these norms and violates a wide range of articles in the Bill of Rights.

In the next chapter, we shall go into the different articles. What we shall do here is discuss the criteria that all laws must comply with and present a principled position against drug prohibition. We just mentioned a test of reason, and to understand how it invalidates the drug law, remember that the individual is to have as much freedom, responsibility, and self-determination as possible. In order to justify any limitation on our freedoms, therefore, the State must prove that "just requirements of morality, public order, and the general welfare" dictate restrictions.

This means that the law must satisfy the test of legality,

necessity, reasonableness, and legitimate purpose. To succeed in this endeavor, responsible officials must show that a separation between licit and illicit drugs makes sense and that there are good reasons for criminalizing illicit drug users. The only way to do this is to demonstrate in specific fashion the precise nature of the threat (i.e., the illicit drugs). Then, the State must show that the drug law is necessary to combat this threat; that it is effective in doing so; and that it at the same time preserves the interests of the individual and society.

This means that a prohibition must not only be effective in curbing the supply and demand of illicit drugs, but that it must be *the least intrusive* instrument amongst those which might achieve a protective function. *All these criteria must be met*, because only so can prohibitionists demonstrate that the law strikes a fair balance between the rights of the individual and the interests of the community. This is the essence of the test of reason and if the State fails to show that the drug law meets these criteria, we have an arbitrary, disproportionate, and discriminatory practice—and a violation of rights.

That said, we shall have a look at principles of equality and proportionality. These principles are key to understand rights; they shape and bring life to most enumerated rights, and we shall see how they invalidate the drug law.

# 3. 1. 1. The Equality Principle and the Drug Law

> *"To cheapen the lives of any group of men, cheapens the lives of all men, even our own. This is a law of human psychology, or human nature. And it will not be repealed by our wishes, nor will it be merciful to our blindness."*
>
> *—William Pickens, author—*

This principle is articulated in ICCPR Articles 2 (1) and 26, and is a key pillar of human rights law.[*] It is relevant because (1) we have divided drugs into two categories; (2) there is no good reason that can explain why some drugs are legal while others are prohibited;[11] and (3), in all cases, a health-oriented approach towards users is the most sensible strategy.[12] Still, while we grant such an approach to the users of tobacco and alcohol, we have policies that deny the same to the users of cannabis and cocaine. And this being so, we have a violation of Article 26.

That illegal drugs pose no greater threat than legal drugs is not likely to appease prohibitionists. In their minds, every measure should be taken to protect us against the illegal drugs, and they believe the drug laws to be an indispensable tool.

---

[*] This principle is a fundamental part of the International Bill of Human Rights. In the Universal Declaration of Human Rights, we find it alluded or referred to in articles 1, 2, 3, 6, 7, 8, 10, 21 (2), 23 (2). In the Charter it is found in the preamble, as well as articles 1 (2), 1 (3) and 55. In the ICCPR the same goes for its preamble and articles 1, 2, 3, 14, 16, 24 and 26.

We shall later see that they overestimate the value of these laws in stemming the flow of drugs and discouraging use. Here, we are concerned with the qualities of the drugs and not the drug laws. And even though the prohibitionists oppose an overall drug policy that does not rely on punitive measures, their fears are misplaced. Indeed, when we compare the legal and illegal drugs, our drug policies are completely backward, as we have chosen to criminalise *the least dangerous* ones.

That alcohol and tobacco are the most dangerous drugs is not generally known. We are born into a world where we have normalised relations with the users of these drugs, and even though there are risks involved, we do not elevate danger to the point where the legal drugs—in our minds—can compare to the illegal drugs. In fact, many people do not think of alcohol and tobacco as drugs. Instead, "drugs" is a catch-all phrase for the illegal substances; those that authorities connect to a life of crime and misery. And while most can appreciate that there is a difference between the use and misuse of alcohol, and that this substance can offer good as well as bad experiences, authorities refuse to acknowledge the same thinking when it comes to illegal drugs. Instead, *all illegal drug use* equals misuse and all illegal drug experiences are suspect.

Such lore is part of the propaganda that is propagated by authorities to win hearts and minds. Most officials probably believe in their quest, but it is easy to see their delusion.

After all, anyone familiar with illegal drugs knows that their addictive nature, as well as every other danger associated with them, is greatly exaggerated. They also know that effects vary according to dosage and that, just like alcohol drinkers, the majority is thankful for their experience. In fact, like alcohol drinkers, 90 percent of illicit drug users[13] do not develop a problematic drug relationship—and even those who do, have a love/hate relationship.

Our leaders, for their part, will not admit to any of this. They have been waging a war against drugs and their users for some time and if the enemy did not turn out to be as bad as they thought, the righteousness of their crusade would have to be reconsidered. This they will not risk. As previously discussed, all bureaucracies seek to expand their influence, and after decades of drug war the costs of admitting defeat have become too great to consider. Systemwise, therefore, mechanisms ensure that civil servants whose primary concern is to help this force feed itself (by enlarging the power and budgets of their organization vis-à-vis other competing agencies and the population) are promoted.

This explains our leaders' unwillingness to reconsider the appropriateness of their war effort, as well as the system's way of dealing with "deserters". As the American author Upton Sinclair once said, "it is difficult for a man to understand something when his salary depends upon his not understanding it." And so, our leaders, over a period of 60 years, have ignored the increasing evidence that prohibition policies, built on totalitarian premises, make everything worse.

We shall have more to say on this. But to preserve false doctrines, prohibitionists have relied on propaganda to obscure the facts.[14] None of the government-funded researchers, for instance, have addressed the most obvious question of all, *why* we have laws against some drugs and not others. In fact, meaningful comparison between the drugs in the different categories has been avoided. And when forced to reflect upon the popularity of illegal drugs, our leaders have explained it with a combination of the degenerate morality of drug users and the demonic powers of drugs.

This being so, many feel confident that no matter how bad the legal drugs, the illegal ones must be worse. Still, there is evidence to the contrary, and when we look at the statistics that compare the harmfulness of legal and illegal drugs, we find no rational or scientific reasons that can explain *why* some are illegal. The most comprehensive study done on the subject was performed by the Independent Scientific Committee on Drugs (ISCD). And after reviewing 20 of the most commonly used drugs and comparing them to 16 criteria of harm (where 100 was the worst possible outcome, indicating maximum harm, and 0 was the best possible outcome, indicating no harm at all), they came up with the following ranking: Alcohol (72), Heroin (55), Crack (54), Methylamphetamine (33), Cocaine (27), Tobacco (26), Amphetamine (23), Cannabis (20), GHB (19), Benzodiazepines (15), Ketamine (15), Methadone (14), Mephedrone (13), Butane (11), Anabolic Steroids (10), Ecstasy (9), Khat (9), LSD (7), Buprenorphine (7), and Psychedelic mushrooms (6).[15]

As we can see, there is no relation between the overall harmfulness of these drugs and their classification. In fact, in most cases the classification is backwards, being that the least dangerous drugs are classified as the most dangerous in the UN drug control conventions.

Predictably, many people will disagree with the ISCD. That alcohol could be more dangerous than heroin, and that tobacco could be more dangerous than LSD is so contradictory to our common beliefs that quite a few will discard the findings. Still, the evidence is overwhelming: Only double standards and hypocrisy maintains a regime of prohibition. What is worse, these double standards result in arbitrary persecution and imprisonment. This is a violation of human rights—and our officials, if they ignore this evidence, can be held criminally negligent.

That civil servants, in continuing to deny the evidence, are exposed to criminal liability is controversial. Yet, the evidence has been available for at least 40 years, and politicians have tried to suppress it. In fact, it is not a coincidence that the ISCD-study was done by an independent scientific committee. As mentioned, government-funded research has focused on undertakings that were intended to strengthen the myths of prohibition. And when honest researchers have opposed the biased approach, they have frequently been threatened with budgetary cuts or, if this did not work, forced to resign, or fired.

Indeed, it was because of these practices that the ISCD was created. Before taking this job, its leader, the psychiatrist and neuropsychopharmacologist professor David Nutt, was head of ACMD, the British government's advisory council on drug policy. As chair of this body, he advocated a more scientific approach. He criticised the government for ignoring its own advisory council's recommendations, and after stating that cannabis was a less harmful drug than alcohol and that the use of ecstasy was a less dangerous activity than horse riding, he was fired. As a consequence, a handful ACMD advisors resigned in protest, and the ISCD came into being. This committee has since been an important promoter of evidence-based drug policies, and Nutt has published a book that fully supports the case we are about to make. As Nutt describes his view of current policies: "[I am] critical of the 'War on drugs', not just because this set of policies has caused enormous damage to millions of people around the world, but also because the evidence of the harm it has been causing hasn't led to a change of approach."[16]

We shall soon see more to the harms of prohibition. But there is more to say on the classification system that serves to uphold current policies, and if it is hard to believe that we have legalised the most dangerous drugs, a look at the death statistics may help. As Nutt says: "Each year tobacco kills 5 million people across the world, while alcohol kills 1, 5 million. By comparison, illicit drugs kill around 200,000 people between them. Even taking into account the much smaller populations who use these drugs, in many cases they are considerably less deadly."[17]

A study by the British medical journal *Lancet* has more to say, and after looking at the number of users per drug-related death in Britain, it concluded with the following list: Tobacco (87 users per death); Street Methadone (111 users per death); Benzodiazepines/Valium (246 users per death); Heroin (428 users per death); Solvents (545 users per death); Alcohol (1000 users per death); Cocaine (3644 users per death); Amphetamine (12.285 users per death); Ecstasy (18.518 users per death).

Notice that drugs like cannabis, LSD, ketamine, and khat are missing from this list even though they are quite popular. The reason is that the numbers of deaths associated with their use are too few to count. Granted, there are more that can be said about this list, one criticism being that it only refers to British people's patterns of drug use. Nonetheless, we see that tobacco is the leading death-agent by far, and while the licit drugs combined kill about 155,000 Britons, the illicit drugs taken together kill roughly 1000 a year.

Now, we just saw Nutt attribute 200,000 deaths worldwide to the illicit drugs[*]. Even if this is less than the approximately 300,000 deaths which each year, according to American doctors[18], are caused by prescription drugs in the U.S. alone, this is quite a lot. Still, most of these 200,000 deaths are not attributable to the inherent qualities of the drugs, but to prohibition. For instance, when we take a closer look at the 25,000 deaths that the National Institute of Drug Abuse (NIDA) lists as a result of illicit drug abuse in the U.S., 14.300 are due to hepatitis and AIDS, diseases that are not caused by illicit drugs, but by the dirty needles that heroin addicts tend to share.[19]

There is also a myriad of other ways by which prohibition kills. The point here is to bring this fact into the equation, and if there is anything wrong with the ISCD's ratings, it is that the illegal drugs are disadvantaged by their mere status.

The ISCD evaluated the dangers of these drugs as they

---

[*] This could be an exaggeration as, according to the WHO, there were 157,800 deaths attributed to illicit drugs (all causes) in 2010.

appear under prohibition, and because their destructive power results from their illicit status, it is not a fair assessment. After all, when it comes to heroin, to quote Brechter, there is "general agreement throughout the medical and psychiatric literature that the overall effects of [this drug] on the users' mind and body under conditions of low price and ready availability are on the whole amazingly bland."[20] And if it were not for the regrettable mechanisms of prohibition, opiate addiction would have been a lot less problematic for both drug users and society.[21]

How much less problematic is impossible to predict. But we see that methadone scores only 14 points on ISCD's rating on overall harm and this is indicative. Many people consider this drug to be more addictive than heroin and since it is also more harmful, heroin would, under legal circumstances, rate even lower.

Again, this reasoning is difficult for prohibitionists to understand. They are used to seeing heroin as the most destructive drug of all, and they do not understand that everything they associate with the life of an addict (the crime, the prostitution, the sickness, the lifestyle, the overdoses) is the result of prohibition—and not the drug itself. Still, the evidence is unambiguous, and there is no doubt that our drug laws represent a discriminatory practice.

Some may argue that this is OK. After all, the human rights conventions do not explicitly grant us a "right to use drugs" nor do they openly prohibit discriminating practices in drug policy. This counter-offensive from prohibitionists, however, will not stand up to scrutiny, as the principle of non-discrimination is of *a general character*. The UN Human Rights Committee has said as much:

*"The committee believes that the term 'discrimination' as used in the Covenant should be understood to imply any distinction, exclusion, restriction or preference which is based on any ground such as race, colour, sex, language, religion, political or other opinion, natural or social origin, property, birth or other status, and which has the purpose or effect of nullifying or impairing the recognition, enjoyment or exercise by all persons on an equal footing, of all rights and freedoms."[22]*

The Committee then goes on to say that:

*"[Article 26] prohibits discrimination in law or in fact in any field regulated and protected by public authorities. [It] is therefore concerned with the obligations imposed on State's parties in regard to their legislation and the application thereof. Thus, when legislation is adopted by a State party, it must comply with the requirement of Article 26 that its content should not be discriminatory. In other words, the application of the principle of non-discrimination contained in Article 26 is not limited to those rights which are provided for by the Covenant."[23]*

As we can see, the Committee has taken a broad view of this provision, relating it to all provisions of law, and it is adamant that all "distinctions drawn by law must be based upon reasonable and objective grounds."[24] Hence, there can be no doubt that the principle of non-discrimination also must be applied to the field of drug policy—and now that we have established this, it is time to bring the proportionality principle into the equation.

## 3. 1. 2. The Proportionality Principle

*"The state should be able to demonstrate that it has good reasons and has proceeded rationally and with attention to the adequacy of less rights-invasive alternatives before putting a person in jail. Proportionality holds the promise of ridding the criminal law of irrational, arbitrary, and unnecessary restrictions on the negative liberty of accused persons. . . . Proportionality is the discipline that constitutional law can bring to the criminal law."[25]*

*—Kent Roach, Professor of Law—*

This principle is another important pillar of human rights.[*]

---

[*] Like the equality principle, it is a fundamental part of the Bill of Rights: in the Universal Declaration of Human Rights, we find it implicit or referred to in articles 9, 12, 15, 17 (2), 29 (2). In the ICCPR, the same applies to articles 2, 4 (1), 5, 6 (1), 7, 9 (1), 11, 12 (3), 17 (1), 18 (3), 19 (3), 21, 22.

And being interlinked with the equality principle, we need to take a look at it when we are to determine our drug laws' relationship to human rights.

The reason is that the conventions do not prohibit unequal treatment per se. And when we think of it, there are many examples where the State has adopted a certain set of policies for one segment of the population and another for the rest: tourists or refugees, for example, do not enjoy the same catalogue of rights as natural citizens, and minorities may receive preferential treatment.

These policies are within the limits of human rights law as they have a purpose and an objective which is legitimate under the conventions. As the Human Rights Committee put it: "the principle of equality sometimes requires State's parties to take affirmative action in order to diminish or eliminate conditions which cause or help to perpetuate discrimination prohibited by the Covenant."[26]

Consequently, the only differential treatment that the Human Rights conventions frown upon are those "distinctions, exclusions, restrictions, or preferences . . . which has the purpose or effect of nullifying or impairing the recognition, enjoyment, or exercise, on an equal footing, of human rights and fundamental freedoms"[27] in any area of public life.

If our leaders therefore can speak coherently as to *why* we, as a society, should treat the users of heroin and cannabis differently than users of alcohol and tobacco, the drug laws are compatible with human rights law—and they are free to continue a regime of prohibition. It comes down to this simple question. Even so, as Douglas Husak, a professor of law, concludes after reviewing their arguments: "Many attempts to answer this question have been made; none is persuasive."[28]

This being so, we are dealing with a violation of the equality principle.

But one might ask, what if our leaders were to criminalise drugs like tobacco and alcohol? Would a regime of prohibition then be okay? The discriminatory aspect would no longer apply, so is it possible to continue with prohibition provided we criminalize all drugs?

The answer is no. And the reason is the principle of proportionality. To elaborate, we live in a society which aims to offer the individual as much control over his/her own life as possible. This principle is at the basis of our contract with the State, and our constitutions, as well as the Bill of Rights, are a testimony to this. We therefore can measure the State's legitimacy according to this standard and to the degree it knows its place vis-à-vis the individual.

Unfortunately, however, states have not wanted a balance. After all, such a balance is only achievable in a society where every individual is seen as equally important and the State is equally concerned with protecting/enhancing the life, rights, and dignity of each and every one of its citizens, regardless of class distinctions.

Our leaders, of course, will profess that this is the case. States have embraced such notions not only intellectually but legally in their commitment to the human rights apparatus. To admit that it in fact was not so, therefore, would be to admit that the State did not comply with its obligations, and our leaders are not likely to do this. No matter how bad their human rights record, therefore, they will, like they have done for centuries, argue that whatever law they enact is for the good of the nation.

Still, it is not always so, as governments are not the benevolent instruments of reason that they pretend to be. Even if we have come a long way since the old days when kings had a divine right to rule; the aristocracy had rights according to their wealth and status; and the people were left with no rights at all, we still have not matured to the point where we, as a society, can live up to the standards we have set for ourselves. It is in name only that we have a government of the people, by the people, and for the people, and in reality, the state apparatus is a conglomerate of powerful and competing factions struggling to enlarge their influence on the body politic.

This, of course, is a simplification. But we still live in a hierarchical society where certain elite groups have a lot more influence over the political process than any array of ordinary citizens could dream of exercising. These elite groups are mostly concerned with protecting their own special interests, and as a result the state apparatus becomes a machine that the most powerful groups seek to control in order to maximise their influence and realise short-sighted ambitions. So it has been for centuries, and so it is today. And as long as it remains so, the state apparatus will expand its reach according to the ambitions of these special interests.

Now, the only way for such a dynamic to unfold is for the State to adopt and enforce such policies that restrict the fundamental freedoms of ordinary citizens. It is no coincidence that drug prohibition has been a boon to profiteers of war, and I have seen 3-year-olds connect the dots between war profiteers and politicians. Only most adults ignore this connection. Even so, we have seen that the only way a government can enlarge its freedom of action is to reduce the freedom of the individual. And the Bill of Rights, therefore, in recognizing this fact, provides us with a yardstick intended to protect us from undue restrictions placed upon the individual by authoritarian State laws.

This yardstick is expressed in the equality and proportionality principle. As mentioned, there is a presumption of liberty, and Article 29 (2) of the Universal Declaration elaborates on the standards that all laws must comply with:

*"In the exercise of his rights and freedoms everyone shall be subject only to such limitations as are determined by law solely for the purpose of securing due freedoms of others and of meeting the just requirements of morality, public order and the general welfare in a democratic society."*

As we can see, for a law to be acceptable its purpose must be to protect our rights of person (our right to life, liberty, and the pursuit of happiness) and property against injustices forced upon us by others, and the restriction must be no more repressive than absolutely necessary for the general welfare of a democratic society. This idea of justice is straightforward and thinkers like Spencer, Kant, Mill, and Rawls have elaborated upon this basis.

Our laws, in other words, shall be *a mutual protection against injustice*. And when prohibitionists defend the drug laws according to these criteria, their argument is that the illegal drugs present such a threat that the drug law is necessary not only to save the individual from himself, but his surroundings from the dehumanising and demoralising effects these drugs have on his person. They feel confident that without prohibition, society would not function, and so they have no problem believing that these laws are compatible with the provisions raised by the principle of proportionality. After all, no matter how bad it is, they will argue that without these laws everything would be worse. And so, when confronted with the yardsticks[*] of the proportionality principle, they will in all cases argue "yes", believing that all things considered, the drug laws strike a fair balance between the rights of the individual and the interests of society.

As we shall see, they are misguided. But before we elaborate on the drug laws' conflict with the proportionality principle, we need to look at their consequences.

---

[*] These are key questions: (1) is there a legitimate aim to the interference; (2) is the measure suitable or appropriate to achieve the desired end; and (3) is the interference proportionate to the identified aim and necessary in a democratic society.

### 3. 1. 3. Our Drug Laws' Destructive Effects

*"Liberty has never come from government. Liberty has always come from the subjects of government. The history of liberty is the history of resistance."*[29]


*—Woodrow Wilson, U.S. President—*


We have seen that the illicit drugs are far less dangerous to the user and society than the prohibitionists can imagine. It should therefore be obvious that if the regulated supply of drugs like alcohol and tobacco has not already brought our civilization to its knees, there is no reason to believe that the regulated supply of other drugs will.

This simple reasoning, unfortunately, have not convinced prohibitionists. Despite the evidence, they insist that the illegal drugs are exceptionally dangerous, and they rarely listen to those of other opinions. This explains why they do not see the similarities between the 1920s' alcohol prohibition and today's narcotics prohibition. And it also explains why our leaders, while agreeing that alcohol prohibition was a failed social experiment which no one seriously considers returning to, in their next breath—and with a straight face—will argue the exact opposite when it comes to our experiment with drug prohibition.

Still, the lesson is obvious. And for those with eyes to see, the explanations of why we should not return to a prohibition of alcohol also applies to other drugs. After all, the problems caused by alcohol prohibition were infinitesimal compared to what has manifested in the wake of narcotics prohibition. It is the same phenomenon, only intensified, and the reason is that humanity is one giant organism. What we do to others have consequences to ourselves, and as the war on drugs/ alcohol is nothing but a war on human nature, it should be obvious that the harder we fight this war, the more we will lose. It is that simple. The history of prohibition reflects this fact and so, as alcohol prohibition was a "light-version" of our fight today, its destructive consequences was nothing compared to the war on drugs.

When it comes to alcohol prohibition, the law-and-order approach was much less repressive; the budgets that went to enforcement were comparatively small, punishment for violating the law was rare, people could drink in their home, and few smugglers or sellers went to jail for any length of time. Still, the criminalization created many problems. As one would expect, the black market brought a sharp rise in alcohol-related death and disease. And while having to buy their goods from gangsters who sometimes sold them poisonous drink was a problem for users, the underground economy became society's great challenge. As historian Hugh brogan said:

*"The price of official righteousness always comes high and in case of alcohol prohibition some $2 billion worth of business was transferred from brewers and bar-keepers to bootleggers and gangsters who worked in close co-operation with the policemen and politicians*

Alcohol prohibition, therefore, was our politicians' gift to organized crime. Failing to stop demand or obstruct the supply chain, all it did was to undermine the authority of law, and yet this is nothing compared to narcotics prohibition. After all, while alcohol prohibition was a limited national effort which lasted a mere decade before politicians put an end to it, drug prohibition is a worldwide effort which has been given free and expansive rein for more than 50 years.

Looking back, the budgets spent fighting this war are measured in trillions of dollars. Still, we are no closer to controlling the supply or the demand side of the illicit drug trade. Instead, on the supply side, drugs are not only more available but cheaper and of better quality than before,[31] while on the demand side, drug use is more widespread and socially accepted.[32] In other words, the war on drugs, in its own terms, has failed.

We must not forget that it was the supply and demand that the law-and-order approach was supposed to attack. And yet it has proven to be a completely dysfunctional venture. After all, we are further away from the ideal of a drug-free society than ever. Instead, prohibition has enabled destructive mechanisms to thrive, and even though we shall not go into this at length, a brief summarization of the side-effects of prohibition will look like this:

➤ The war on drugs has created an enormous underground economy which every year generates $400-700 billion in profits.

➤ This economy has given rise to the greatest criminal enterprise the world has ever seen.

➤ Organised crime does not exist in a vacuum; it can only expand at the expense of the rule of law, and its corruptive influence is threatening to undermine the government and stability of nations.

➤ The underground economy is controlled by intelligence agencies, warlords, and shady elites.[*] These anti-social forces depend on this economy to feed their own ambitions and the profits generated from the drug trade are spent on terror operations, as well as other warfare.

➤ In the drugs economy there is no law-and-order to settle disputes. Instead, people are left to fend for themselves and the most cynical and ruthless individuals come out on top.

➤ This makes threats, bribery, kidnappings, violence, and murder commonplace. And although it is impossible to estimate or imagine the suffering and hardships that is generated by this regime, millions have died because of

---

[*] For more on powerpolitics and drugs, see MIKALSEN, *HUMAN RISING* (2021), part three.

the underground economy.[33]

> People in general have too much faith in authority. They rarely know how to question the legitimacy of laws and so foolish and inhumane laws produce foolish and inhumane societies. To prohibitionists, the drug law represents everything they hold dear, and so violators come to represent the opposite. They become the fiends, the problems that must be dealt with.

> The drug laws therefore create mechanisms that increase hostilities. To prohibitionists, drug users symbolize everything that is wretched and evil, and they are treated as public enemies. The drug users, in turn, react defensively, returning the contempt and hatred that they are exposed to.

> Thus, drug laws breed not only discrimination, violence, and death, but ignorance, estrangement, and fear. They disengage a deeper morality and professionals have noted the scapegoating phenomenon behind our willingness to embrace drug prohibition. Any reliable government would work to end such a mechanism. Our eagerness to blame minorities for problems that are a collective responsibility is the engine that has ensured human rights violations to this day; from the Spanish Inquisition to the persecution of Jews and Jim Crow laws, drug prohibition is the historical equal to campaigns that we remember as great crimes against

humanity; only unconsciousness and a moral panic can sustain the popularity of this quest, and yet our leaders continue to encourage double standards.

- ➢ A government devoted to policies that depend upon moral panic to survive will have no choice but to use its propaganda apparatus to dumb people down.

- ➢ This is what our governments have done. To justify the persecution of large segments of the population, officials have relied on moral panic and an oversized enemy image to maintain policies that make everything worse. They have disregarded evidence to the contrary, only to encourage ignorance and fear. In doing so, they have disgraced themselves and done a great disservice to the people. But they have also violated ICCPR Article 18, which protects our freedom of thought, as well as Article 20, which holds that "any propaganda for war shall be prohibited by law."

- ➢ The drug laws do not only corrupt the fibre of society by creating a giant underground economy and relying on an exaggerated enemy image to maintain a state of moral panic. As discussed, a bureaucracy's primary concern is maintaining or enlarging its budgets and its sphere of influence, and so the trillions of dollars spent on a war on drugs have had an unfortunate effect. It has encouraged the worst tendencies inherent in the State.

- The logical conclusion to be drawn from the mechanism above will be that the police, as an agency of the State, will strive towards the creation of a police state. This, of course, is a taboo. Nonetheless, history confirms it, and the trillions of dollars allocated to the drug warriors have nurtured a totalitarian state.

- A drug policy on totalitarian premises have not yielded beneficial result. Many experts have noted a connection between increased police efforts, violence, and death. And the overall finding is that the harder we fight the drug war, the worse are the ramifications.

- Thus, as experts confirm,[34] the only segments of society which has thrived on drug laws are war profiteers and organised crime. These forces have a common interest in maintaining the status quo, and as a result ordinary citizens and defenders of a free and open society have been under attack from both.

- This dynamic explains why our drug laws are a threat to civilization. Politicians, gangsters, cops, and other war profiteers all have a common interest in disregarding the rule of law. And as long as these laws exist, these destructive forces will gain momentum and destroy what is left of our open and free society.

- People tend not to notice this drift, because the transfer from a society governed by the rule of law to a police state is gradual. The transfer to a police state, therefore, goes unnoticed and neither the populace nor public officials object to it.

➢ Still, the evidence is there. And while the war on drugs has been a gross failure as measured by its explicitly stated goal (a drug-free world), it has succeeded in demolishing our catalogue of rights and fundamental freedoms.[35]

➢ In fact, at no point in history have government been so meddlesome in our lives; never have so many been imprisoned, and never have we so willingly surrendered to the strong arm of the State.

➢ The enemy image of "drugs" has been used with such precision that it has destroyed our ability to think. So dumbed down and so afraid have we become that the majority accepts the idea that we must give up our freedoms in exchange for security. We have clearly forgot the founders' warning that those who consent to such folly, "deserves neither freedom nor security and shall soon lose both."

➢ Indeed, we have. And we are stuck with an oversized government apparatus consisting of incompetent and corrupt officials who are not content with being mere civil servants. Instead, they think it their right to meddle with the most intimate aspects of our lives—our own consciousness—and when people complain about arbitrary persecution, seeking recourse in the Bill of Rights, they are denied an effective remedy.[*]

> In other words, it is clear that giving up our freedoms, as the founding fathers promised, was a one-way deal. And our lack of vigilance has ensured that we are less secure than ever.

> The politically expedient search for enemies, real and imagined, has not only increased unaccountability and instability in political and social systems, but it has taken its toll on ecosystems and financial systems.

> Another side-effect is that the criminalisation of drugs has increased harm to users.[36] Buying on the black market, people never know what to expect, and the result is more health-related problems, death, and overdoses.

> The criminalisation creates problematic patterns of drug use. One reason is the "Iron Law of Prohibition." Coined by historian Richard Cowan, it states that as the enforcement of prohibited drugs increases, the potency of those drugs increases as well. As a result, heroin and cocaine becomes readily available, while the less harmful version of these drugs (opium and coca leaf) is difficult to find.

---

[*] For more on how governments have failed to honor the rule of law, see archive at www. arodpolicies.org

➢ Another reason for the unfortunate patterns of drug use is that there is no information from authorities on the proper use of illicit drugs. As a result, people are more likely to experiment in senseless ways.

➢ These dynamics lead to an increased spread of infectious disease. Hence, drug use and sharing needles is now the cause of one out of three new instances of HIV/Aids in the world, except for the area south of Sahara.[37]

➢ Another problem with prohibition reasoning is that it presents the user as a mindless victim overwhelmed by the power of drugs. The user himself is prone to accept such myths and so chances are (1) that he will use these drugs less responsibly; (2) that he will more easily become addicted; (3) that he will more likely stay addicted; and (4) that he will be encouraged to blame the drug, rather than himself.

➢ The criminalisation exposes drug users to a downward spiral being that they are, by definition, criminals and must deal with other criminals. If, for example, they end up owing money or otherwise cannot afford their habits, they are likely to become dealers themselves or engage in other criminal activities to survive.

➢ Prohibition, in other words, generates *a lot* of crime.[38]

- The backwards classification between licit and illicit drugs have not only created irrational fears; it has diverted attention from the dangers of alcohol and tobacco, as most people are under the impression that these drugs are less harmful.

- Quite a few drugs (e.g., cannabis, heroin, cocaine, LSD, mushrooms, amphetamines, ecstasy) have medical properties, and prohibition ensures that they remain unavailable for legitimate use.

- The criminalisation of such drugs has held back medical research.

- It has also caused millions of terminally ill to die in needless agony because doctors are afraid to lose their licence—or go to jail—if they prescribe effective pain medicine.

- The criminalisation of these drugs has forced people to use prescription drugs which in many cases are worse than the illicit ones—and less effective.

- There is a blurry line between medical and recreational use. Most recreational use can be considered medical being that it makes us happier, more focused, more content, more comfortable, more relaxed, less in pain, etc.

- Separating medical and recreational use not only makes no sense, but it has made it impossible to deal with pain and illnesses.

- In fact, it is a curious coincidence that we have outlawed the same drugs that people have used to heal themselves for thousands of years. And that we in criminalising self-medication—which was the norm until the 20th century—have created a lucrative business for the medical profession and pharmaceutical companies.

- In giving up our right to self-medication, we have given the responsibility for our health to a higher authority. We have done so much in the same way that naïve Christians have given the responsibility for their salvation to the Church, and even though there are good and decent doctors out there (just as there are good and decent priests), this was a foolish thing to do. After all, every time we give our power away, we become a little more enslaved. And we should know by now that whatever class of people we put on a pedestal will take advantage of its position and seek to expand its sphere of influence.

- The result of giving up our power is evident everywhere. We have seen how civil servants have misused the power entrusted to them, but also the medical profession has taken advantage of the drug laws. Rehabilitation clinics, addiction-, maintenance-, and treatment programs are examples of this. And while there are professionals who have had the wisdom and integrity to expose the myths of prohibitionist-lore, most have accepted these myths as truths. For instance, few doctors have opposed the absurdity of classifying all illicit drug use as "misuse." Instead, they have argued for more rehabilitation clinics, and the fact that most people have been forced into these programs on totalitarian grounds have been lost on them.

➢ In addition to this, the addiction maintenance programs are a vulgar practice, as they force users to give up their favourite opiate (heroin) in exchange for another and more harmful drug (methadone). Thomas Szasz, a distinguished professor of psychiatry, noted the absurdity of such practices:

*"The modern zeitgeist [is] our seemingly limitless fear of and faith in drugs. The fear explains our timidity towards opiates; the faith, our belief that the habitual use of one narcotic (heroin) is a disease, which can be successfully treated with another narcotic (methadone). Grounded in pharmacomythology, not pharmacology, these fears and faiths cannot be dispelled by common sense or medical experience. Instead, we live according to the old adage credo quia absurdum est (I believe because it is absurd), which we find comforting because the credo lists the burden of responsibility for our bad habits from our shoulders. Using one narcotic to cure the addict by taking another narcotic authenticates the doctor's expertise about habit-forming and habit-curing*

The sum of all this makes prohibition a failed social experiment. And even though this may be news, these points are no exaggeration. The evidence is available in books, expert testimonies, and reports. Even constitutional courts have begun to invalidate drug laws, and the evidence being unambiguous and overwhelming, officials should recognize the gravity of the status quo.

Not only do they have a duty to provide an effective remedy to the persecuted but police, politicians, courts, and prison authorities, just like everyone else, would be better off without these laws. Prohibitionists may disagree, but no one is really served by the enforcement of inhumane legislation. And as it has chipped away at such enforcers' credibility for more than 50 years, our officials have an obligation to deal with these alleged human rights violations.

Now bear in mind that this list is not complete. These are just the most obvious side-effects of prohibition, and we have said nothing of the perverse consequences that result from its *explicitly* stated goals—to put drug law violators behind bars.

This consequence of prohibition must be elaborated on, for we should not forget that the criminalisation has deprived a steadily increasing percentage of the population of their freedom. Their numbers are measured in millions, and we have not only made life a living hell for these people, but their families and loved ones. The hardships, the pain, and the suffering these people have had to endure because of prohibition is not only unspeakable but a testimony to the price our officials are willing to pay to preserve their image as crusaders fighting a righteous cause. Imprisonment, after all, is an extremely punitive measure and any decent society would wish to limit its use to a bare minimum.

The reason for this is that prisons are places of destructive mechanisms and to the degree we avoid exposing people to such conditions everybody will be better off. Our willingness to expose non-violent people to such hardships is therefore the most visible and concrete example of how prohibition destroys our morality. After all, very few have opposed this regime of mass-incarceration, and empathy with these inmates would be weird to prohibitionists.

The reason is that they are overwhelmed by the power of an exaggerated enemy image and have lost their ability to put two and two together. We have already been introduced to their confused reasoning: As they see the world, drug users are the victims of an evil which threatens to destroy us all. In their minds, therefore, these people should be thrown in prison or forced into rehabilitation camps for their own good. And while they may have some pity with these "victims", the people who provide them with their drug of choice are the ultimate enemy. Consequently, many countries have death penalties for drug dealing and even if authorities in more civilized parts of the world do not go that far, they deal out sentences which are more severe than those offered to murderers and rapists. The viciousness and manifest absurdity of such laws is lost because, according to a prohibitionist's thought, the victims of their trade are measured in the millions.

Nevertheless, it is the same law of supply and demand involved when it comes to legal and illegal drugs. This is difficult for prohibitionists to comprehend. But if they did, they would recognise the policies they have been supporting for what they are. It would then be clear to them that the drug law violators, those "evil and cynical dealers in death", were in fact no more cynical and depraved than anyone involved with the supply-chain of alcohol and tobacco. And that they just as well, therefore, could support criminal policies which sought to put people like this (the farmers, the brewers, the truck drivers, the salesmen, the barkeepers, and most likely themselves) behind bars.

This logic is, of course, hard to grasp. But understanding this, the next step is coming to grips with the fact that the drug law enforcers are a lot more "cynical" and "evil" than the drug law violators. While the latter have provided people with a service they want, the drug law enforcers have done so much worse. In their enforcement of these laws, they have tapped people's phones, opened their mail, spied on them, searched their houses, stripped them naked, performed cavity searches, fined them, confiscated their property and their valuables, forced them into "rehabilitation", jailed them, taken their children from them, destroyed their education and work possibilities. In short, they have threatened, humiliated, beaten, demonised, discriminated, stigmatised, terrorised, and shot at drug law violators for nearly a century—and finally, when the persecuted have had enough of such affairs and wanted an effective remedy, they have set aside the rule of law to perpetuate unlawful and unjust policies.

This, I am sure, may be tough words to hear. Nevertheless, it is an accurate description. And even though this may leave an unflattering image of prohibitionists, their only sin is falling prey to an oversized enemy image—and that is all it takes to take part in such practices.

In fact, when we look at history, it is the same story behind every war and atrocity: Proponents of the inquisition were convinced that Satan lived inside those who did not conform to their way of life; the Nazis saw the Jews as a threat against their state; Muslim fundamentalists see the West as an immense evil and corrupt force which threaten all that is dear, and Christian fundamentalists think exactly the same—just the other way around.

No matter where we look, it is the same. And behind every war and atrocity, we find an enemy image which seemed to validate the belief that the ends justify the means. The war on drugs, in this regard, is no different than any other war. And as we are born into a society at war with itself, it is only natural that most fall prey to the sloppy thinking that got us into this mess (what John Stuart Mill called the despotism of custom). Most people, after all, start out with a presumption that we are part of a decent society and that our leaders are intelligent people who want what is best for us. No matter time and place, this basic assumption is widely shared. Our upbringing and our education seem to confirm this, and so we take for granted that wars are fought for some greater good and that laws are in place for good reasons.

It is only with experience that we grow wiser. And so,

some people find that the drugs they have been raised to fear are not what they have been taught; that they in most cases provide people with an experience they find pleasant; and that the war on drugs, on the other hand, is a highly unpleasant and destructive campaign which is only desirable to gangsters and war profiteers. In other words, it becomes obvious that they had it all wrong and that their leaders—the proponents of this war—are not the good guys.

This is the real reason why President Nixon hated drug users. People in power know that drug use is connected to rebellion because it makes people see authority more clearly, and as the faith in authority is weakened, people break free from the old paradigm. That is the real threat of drugs. Drug users are the first to notice the fallacies of the status quo and the most likely to oppose the union between crime and government. Being involved with the black market, the old world of black and white begins to crumble and drug users see the shades of grey. They start thinking about the enormity of the drug trade and the fact that, together with oil and arms, it is the world's biggest commercial enterprise; they begin to imagine what this economy of some $400-700 billion a year does to society; the corruptive influence it must have, and how many politicians, judges, policemen, bureaucrats, agencies, banks, and intelligence services which are part of it.

Drug users think about this more than anyone else. And it does not take much study before they realise that tens of trillions of dollars have been laundered by our banks and that no one has gone to jail for this. Thus, it dawns on them that the black and white economy is not separate and that drug barons like Pablo Escobar are not at the top of the food-chain. Instead, people like him turn out to be players in a greater game of shadows where the secret services rule supreme, deeply involved in shaping all aspects of the enormous market to suit the needs and ambitions of elite masters.

This line of thinking is much more likely to manifest among drug users. Being the black sheep of society, they learn more about society than anyone else, and as they investigate our leaders' stated reasons for going to war, they find that their pretexts are lies and double standards. They reflect upon this fact and are bound to notice that, even though these falsehoods are easily exposed, few cares to dig for truth. Instead, the major players in academia, media, and even in the political opposition parties, seem more concerned with burying the facts. This at first may puzzle drug users. But the drug war continues. Years go by, and as their vision expand and they watch the power of elites, they begin to see war differently; they realize that war is not some benevolent attempt to spread freedom and democracy or a fight for the greater good, but that it conforms to historic precedent and power-political reasons.[40] This means that the engine of war has always been the urge of elites to (1) take control of resources abroad and (2) to strengthen control of populations at home.

Accepting this, drug users are prone to rationalize that maybe the war on drugs is not a result of ignorant thinking; maybe politicians do not mind the scapegoating and the destructive social mechanisms; maybe they could care less if the threat of "drugs" is exaggerated; maybe they have no problem if the credibility the drug law depends upon a moral panic and that the enemy image destroys our ability to think. Could it, when all is said and done, be that the wide range of side-effects are not unintended? Could the fight against drugs be a charade, a campaign whose real purpose is to keep doing what it does—fill the pockets of war-profiteers, while feeding those mechanisms that undermine our liberties and keep them in power?

Such reasoning, of course, is just silly to prohibitionists. They are still under the spell of an oversized enemy image and having kept their faith in authority, they see the world in black and white. Consequently, to them, their leaders are always good, their enemies always evil, and begging to differ is unpatriotic.

Still, there is evidence to the contrary. And the more we learn, the more pressing such thinking becomes. This is the real threat not only of drugs, but of the drug war. It exposes everyone involved to its hypocrisy, and so also drug warriors have proven a nuisance. Just as drug users, they have a front-row seat to the destructiveness of the drug war, and after fighting the war for years, they begin to understand that it is not about ridding the streets of drugs, but a matter of budgets, power, and careers. It is just more difficult for the oppressor than the victim to put two and two together, and so most will continue to blame drug dealers. Even so, while a majority, in doing so, finds the moral ground to support a regime of prohibition, a minority understands that they could just as well be arresting bar keepers and that there is a need to change the law. Hence, organizations like Law Enforcement Against Prohibition (LEAP) come into existence, and cops like

Celerino Castillo, Mike Ruppert, and Michael Levine write books about the CIA's involvement in keeping a drug market going. The longer the war goes on, the bigger the opposition against it becomes, but still the war continues.

So it is that more and more begin to speculate that, perhaps, the purpose of this war is not a drug-free world. Perhaps it is no coincidence that the great heroes of prohibition have been bigots with no loyalty to principled law, and that, instead, the whole point is war for war's sake—an eternal war for eternal peace. After all, our leaders cannot honestly believe in their policies; they have been caught too many times burying, faking, distorting, and manipulating the evidence—everything to fit their agenda for war.[41] And while they stand before us as warmongers, in private they often agree that the war effort has failed.[42] Julian Chritchley, a former director of the UK Anti-Drug Coordination Unit confirms:

*"What [I think] was truly depressing about my time in the civil service was that the professionals I met from every sector held the same view: the illegality of drugs causes far more problems for society and the individual than it solves. Yet, publicly, all those people were forced to repeat the mantra that the government would be "tough on drugs", even though they all knew that the policy was causing harm."[43]*

Chritchley quit his job because he "was sick of having to implement policies that I knew, and my political masters knew, were unsupported by evidence."[44] And as any thinking person knows this for a fact, we are left with the conclusion that our leaders must be either (1) hypocrites without a shred of integrity, or (2) people whose ultimate allegiance is to gangsters or war-profiteers. It could be a little bit of both. But either way, it should be obvious that our government has become so corrupted by the drug war that civil servants are either incapable or unwilling to end it. Society has been praying on itself in a collective psychosis for decades. Scapegoating is the engine of drug policy. And as our civil servants, hundreds of times, have proven so eager to keep these policies that they are willing to set aside the rule of law, drug users and human rights defenders can use constitutional rights to fight for an effective remedy.

In chapter 5, we shall elaborate on this bit. We shall now summarize the problems with the principle of proportionality.

## 3. 1. 4. Proportionality and the Drug Law

*"Necessity is the plea for every infringement on human rights. It is the argument of tyrants; it is the creed of slaves."*

*—William Pitt, British Prime Minister—*

From what we have seen, the problems with a principle of proportionality are inferred. After all, while the negative consequences of prohibition are disturbing, they are neither controversial nor disputable. Many—if not most—are in fact acknowledged by prohibitionists. It is just that they will argue that without these laws everything would be worse, and so they believe that it is worth it.

Still, they hold this belief contrary to the evidence. Instead, prohibition has been unsuccessful in curbing the supply and demand of illicit drugs, and there is much to suggest that we would be far better off regulating the sale of these substances. This evidence indicates that the law has failed to deter use.[45] The Netherlands, for example, has sold cannabis products in stores for more than 30 years, but its use is less frequent than in most neighbouring countries—and far less than Americans, who have been subjected to strict penalties.

This evidence is corroborated by other experiments. As of Feb. 2021, 35 U.S. states and the District of Columbia have legalized marijuana use. Canada and many other states have embraced systems of regulation, and when we take this evidence into account, we find that the more we depart from a punitive approach, the better off we are. As Professor Nutt confirms: "Drug users are part of society and when we treat them as such, the outcome improves for everybody, including non-drug users."[46]

In other words, all the damage prohibition has done—all the misery and death that it has caused to violators of the law and all the collateral damage it has caused to society—has been for nothing! And while prohibitionists, to preserve policy, will defend the drug war on the premise that we do not know the consequences of peace, this is a fool's last stand. After all, human rights law is clear, and the burden of evidence is not with proponents of peace. Instead, prohibitionists must justify their reasons for war—and they have never done this.

They have attempted to do so, arguing that the illicit drugs are a threat to our mental health, physical health, moral health, a threat to our children, our community, and so on—and that the law protects us from such harms. These, however, are arguments of faith rather than reason and, as Professor Husak and many others have shown, not very convincing.[47]

In fact, if we stop relying on the exaggerated enemy image that "drugs" represents, we will find that our leaders could just as well criminalize unhealthy foods and throw overweight people in prisons (or forcing them into "rehab"). This, of course, seems absurd. But eating not only provides a "high" which can make people become "addicted": it can lead to serious problems, and health-related issues like diabetes and heart disease kills more people every year than the use of illicit drugs.[48]

Thus, the idea of criminalizing obesity and having the "obesity-police" arrest these people is no more absurd than criminalizing drug users and having the narcotics-police arrest them. I am not advocating either. I am just noting the distasteful stupidity of current policies, and the fact that their impudence is lost on most is a testimony to the power of propaganda.

After all, until a century ago, people would consider the idea of a drug law as an audacity. There were even lawyers who knew how to recognise vices from crimes, a distinction which is lost on most today. Lysander Spooner, a great mind of that age, reminds us of the difference:

> *"Vices are those acts by which a man harms himself or his property. Crimes are those acts by which one man harms the person or property of another. Vices are simply the errors which a man makes in his search after his own happiness. Unlike crimes, they imply no malice towards others, and no interference with their persons or property."*[49]

This is an important distinction to make. We may disagree with other people's lifestyle and think it better if they drank less, spent less time watching TV, playing video games, surfing the internet for porn, and so on. We may prefer that they exercised, ate healthy foods, and cared more for others, but we cannot possibly, in a society governed by the rule of law, enact laws against such behaviours and call them crimes. Spooner explains why:

> *"The object aimed at in the punishment of crimes is to secure, to each and every man alike, the fullest liberty he can possibly have—consistently with the equal right of others—to pursue his own happiness, under the guidance of his own judgment, and by the use of his own property. On the other hand, the object aimed at in the punishment of vices is to deprive every man of his natural right and liberty to pursue his own happiness, under the guidance of his own judgment, and by the use of his own property.*

*These two objects, then, are directly opposed to each other. They are as directly opposed to each other as light and darkness, as truth and falsehood, or as liberty and slavery. They are utterly incompatible with each other; and to suppose the two to be embraced in one and the same government, is an absurdity, an impossibility. It is to suppose the object of a government to be to commit crimes, and to prevent crimes; to destroy individual liberty, and to secure individual liberty.*"[50]

In the 18th century, not only scholars but even politicians recognized this distinction, and a drug law would violate the Constitution. As President Lincoln stated:

*"Prohibition goes beyond the bounds of reason in that it attempts to control a man's appetite by legislation and makes crimes out of things that are not crimes. A prohibition law strikes a blow of the very principles upon which our government was founded.*"[51]

While there are scholars and politicians who recognise this today, we have come a long way. The U.S. Supreme Court has ruled that lifetime imprisonment is not unconstitutionally severe for the possession of cocaine. 33 countries have capital punishment for drug "crimes", and there is no lack of prohibitionists who are prepared to bring us back to the dark ages, advocating corporal punishment to win the war on drugs.

We shall not spend too much time on their reasoning, but

their attitude is exposed by Daryl Gates, who as Chief of Los Angeles Police Department stated that "casual drug users should be taken out and shot. We are in a war and drug use is treason."[52]

As can be seen, prohibitionist propaganda has made a mess. And not only is the distinction between vices and crimes lost, but, as a society, we have lost our way in our sentencing practices. Even if people like Gates belong to the extreme end of the spectrum, there seems to be no end to the lengths most countries will go to punish drug law offenders. And while few jurists can imagine that this constitutes "cruel, inhumane or degrading punishment", hopefully they would reconsider if alcohol drinkers, tobacco farmers, or simply obese people were exposed to such treatment.

After all, from a principled perspective, they have yet to speak coherently when explaining why we should treat illicit drug users any differently than legal drug users. And when it comes to alcohol drinkers, the European Court of Human Rights, in *Witold Litwa v. Polen*, already looked at the principle of proportionality in the area of drug policy.

In this case, the Court considered the appropriateness of putting exceedingly drunk people in prison. It accepted in its verdict that the State could deprive people of liberty if they were a threat to themselves and others, but it concluded that 6.5 hours in a holding cell was an *inappropriate* interference and that it would have been proper to drive Litwa home, to sleep it off in his own bed. It was by any measure a good decision. And while it referred to alcohol users, in a society governed by the rule of law, it would be considered a discriminatory and inappropriate practice to treat illicit drug users any differently.

Now, we all know that reality is not so. Instead, the idea of granting the same rights and the same approach to illicit drug users seems absurd—even objectionable. And so it is that we live in a society, in which each State undertakes to respect and ensure to all individuals—except the drug law violators—the rights recognised in the Bill of Rights; where all persons, except them, shall be equal before the law and be entitled to equal protection of the law; where everybody, except them, shall be recognised as a person before the Courts and entitled to a fair hearing by a competent, impartial and independent tribunal to have their rights determined; where everybody, except them, shall have an effective remedy against unlawful detention and abusive, discriminatory and degrading policies, and where everyone, except them, shall have an enforceable right to compensation after being the victim of such practices.

We live in a society where everybody, except them, shall have the right to self-determination and to pursue their social, cultural, economic, and spiritual development; where every human being, except them, shall have the inherent right to life and to be protected from being arbitrarily deprived of it; where no one, except the drug violators, shall be subjected to cruel, inhuman, or degrading treatment or punishment. Where no one, but them, shall be subjected to arbitrary and unlawful interference with privacy, family, home, or correspondence, and where everyone, but them, have the right to be protected by law against such interferences.

We are to accept a social contract where everyone, except

them, have the right to liberty and security of person and where no one, but them, shall be unlawfully deprived of liberty; where everyone, but them, shall have the right to freedom of expression and to seek, collect, and impart information and ideas of all kinds, regardless of frontiers; where any propaganda for war—except drug war—shall be prohibited by law; where any advocacy of hatred that constitutes incitement to discrimination, hostility, or violence shall be prohibited by law—except that which is directed at drug law violators; and where any family, except theirs, are entitled to protection by society and the State.

While all of this is acceptable to most citizens, it is unfortunate for those who take human rights seriously. After all, there can be no doubt that our drug laws violate of the equality principle. And when it comes to the proportionality principle, these laws have failed scrutiny.

First, we have committed the ultimate stupidity in making a crime out of non-crimes (vices); secondly, the laws intended to deal with these "crimes" have increased harms; and, thirdly, less invasive means are available to achieve the desired ends. In other words, the cure has proven to be worse than the disease; the law therefore is not properly framed, and it cannot be said to strike a fair balance between the rights of the individual and the interests of the community.

According to human rights law, in this situation, there is not a reasonable relationship of proportionality between the aim pursued by prohibition and the means deployed to reach its aim. The drug laws, therefore, cannot be regarded as "necessary in a democratic and open society". On the contrary, these laws are a violence perpetrated against the citizens of the world; they fulfil the criteria to be regarded as a crime against humanity—and the time has come to let the healing begin.

# 4

# The Bill of Rights
# and Prohibition

*"The history of human rights bears a testimony to the evolution and development of human rights as a result of the ever-changing aspirations and needs of people and the ever-increasing need to put constraints on what governments may do to individuals."[53]*

*—B.C. Nirmal, Professor of Law—*

HAVING SEEN HOW drug prohibition fails the test of reason, we shall see how it violates the Bill of Rights[*]. As its articles are interrelated and indivisible, the greater picture is important. Nevertheless, let us begin with article 2 of the Universal

---

[*] As previously stated, the International Bill of Human Rights consists of the Universal Declaration of Human Rights, the International Covenant on Economic, Social and Cultural Rights (ICESCR) and the International Covenant on Civil and Political Rights (ICCPR). While many articles of the ICESCR also can be used to demonstrate a violation, we shall focus on the Universal Declaration of Human Rights and the International Covenant on Civil and Political Rights.

Declaration.

This article holds that "Everyone is entitled to all the rights and freedoms set forth in this Declaration, without distinction of any kind, such as race, color, sex, language, religion, political or other opinion, national or social origin, property, birth or other status."

As we can see, the idea behind this article is to ensure the protection of human rights to every individual. It is a central feature of our catalogue of rights and its implications are elaborated on in ICCPR article 2 (1) which states that "Each State Party to the present Covenant undertakes to respect and to ensure to all individuals within its territory and subject to its jurisdiction the rights recognized in the present Covenant, without distinction of any kind." As we can see, the equality principle is brought into play; *we are all, without distinction of any kind, entitled to the rights and freedoms set forth in this declaration*, and its implications are elaborated on in ICCPR article 2 (2) and 2 (3), which expand on the obligations of the State. These articles emphasize that the State party must take the necessary steps (1) "to ensure that any person whose rights or freedoms as herein recognized are violated shall have an effective remedy"; (2) "to ensure that any person claiming such a remedy shall have his right thereto determined by competent judicial, administrative or legislative authorities, or by any other competent authority provided for by the legal system"; and (3) "to ensure that the competent authorities shall enforce such remedies when granted."

Now, this is important. The State party has a contractual obligation to promote and secure rights, and in its General

Comment no. 31, the Human Rights Committee has more to say on the scope of legal obligations:

> *"The legal obligation under article 2, paragraph 1, is both negative and positive in nature. States Parties must refrain from violation of the rights recognized by the Covenant, and any restrictions on any of those rights must be permissible under the relevant provisions of the Covenant. Where such restrictions are made, States must demonstrate their necessity and only take such measures as are proportionate to the pursuance of legitimate aims in order to ensure continuous and effective protection of Covenant rights. In no case may the restrictions be applied or invoked in a manner that would impair the essence of a Covenant right."*

As we can see, the proportionality principle is key. Recall that the fundamental premise from which all else follows is that the individual is to have as much autonomy as is possible. We find this principle in the Universal Declaration's article 29 (2) which asserts that "In the exercise of his rights and freedoms, everyone shall be subject only to such limitations as are determined by law solely for the purpose of securing due recognition and respect for the rights and freedoms of others and of meeting the just requirements of morality, public order and the general welfare in a democratic society."

ICCPR article 19 (3) also emphasizes this principle. While underlining our right to freedom of expression (our freedom to seek, receive and impart information and ideas of all kinds, regardless of frontiers), it declares:

> *"the exercise of the rights provided for in . . . this article carries with it special duties and responsibilities. It may therefore be subject to certain restrictions, but these shall only be such as are provided by law and are necessary: (a) For respect of the rights or reputations of others; (b) For the protection of national security or of public order, or of public health or morals."*

To justify any limitation on our freedoms, then, the State must prove that "just requirements of morality, public order, and the general welfare in a democratic society" necessitate such action. This means that the drug law must stand the test of reason and that the State must show that (1) there is a legitimate aim to the interference; (2) the measure is suitable or appropriate to achieve the desired end; and (3) that the interference is proportionate to the identified aim and necessary in a democratic society. *Only in doing so can the State party show that a certain limitation satisfies the tests of legality, necessity, reasonableness, and legitimate purpose.* To succeed in this endeavor, the State must (1) show that the drug law does not represent a discriminatory practice, (2) that it is suitable to achieve the desired end (which is a drug-free world), (3) that its interference is proportionate to the identified aim, and (4) that it strikes a fair balance between the rights of the individual and the interests of the community. *If the State fails to show that the drug law meets these criteria, we are dealing with an arbitrary, disproportionate, and discriminatory practice, and we have a violation of our rights.*

To find out if a certain law violates our rights, the State must have the issue reviewed by an independent, impartial, and competent tribunal. Article 2 has more to say. Its paragraph 3 requires that in addition to effective protection of Covenant rights, the State party must ensure that individuals also have accessible and effective remedies to vindicate those rights. The Human Rights Committee's General Comment no. 31 elaborates:

> *"Administrative mechanisms are particularly required to give effect to the general obligation to investigate allegations of violations promptly, thoroughly and effectively through independent and impartial bodies. National human rights institutions, endowed with appropriate powers, can contribute to this end. A failure by a State Party to investigate allegations of violations could in and of itself give rise to a separate breach of the Covenant. Cessation of an ongoing violation is an essential element of the right to an effective remedy."*

Article 2, paragraph 3, requires that States Parties make reparation to individuals whose Covenant rights have been violated, and, when such a violation has occurred, the States must ensure that those responsible are brought to justice. The Human Rights Committee is clear on this. As it continues: "as with failure to investigate, failure to bring to justice perpetrators of such violations could in and of itself give rise to a separate breach of the Covenant." Enforcing accountability is a most serious matter and "where public officials or State agents have committed violations of the Covenant rights referred to in this paragraph, the States Parties concerned may not relieve perpetrators from personal responsibility . . . Furthermore, no official status justifies persons who may be accused of responsibility for such violations being held immune from legal responsibility. Other impediments to the establishment of legal responsibility should also be removed, such as the defense of obedience to superior orders."

*Hence, the provisions of article 2, seek to protect us against all unjust interferences, to provide us with an effective remedy when such interference has occurred, and to hold those officials who are responsible for the violation accountable.*

This is the essence of the Bill of Rights. It is therefore affirmed in a series of articles: In the Universal Declaration of Human Rights, its article 7 holds that "All are equal before the law and are entitled without any discrimination to equal protection of the law. All are entitled to equal protection against any discrimination in violation of this Declaration and against any incitement to such discrimination"; article 8 states that "Everyone has the right to an effective remedy by the competent national tribunals for acts violating the fundamental rights granted him by the constitution or by law"; article 10 affirms that "Everyone is entitled in full equality to a fair and public hearing by an independent and impartial tribunal, in the determination of his rights and obligations and of any criminal charge against him; article 28 says that "Everyone is entitled to a social and international order in which the rights and freedoms set forth in this Declaration can be fully realized"; and article 30 states that "Nothing in this Declaration may be interpreted as implying for any State, group or person any right to engage in any activity or to perform any act aimed at the destruction of any of the rights and freedoms set forth herein."

The importance of an effective remedy is reiterated in the United Declaration's Preamble: "Whereas recognition of the inherent dignity and of the equal and inalienable rights of all members of the human family is the foundation of freedom, justice and peace in the world; Whereas disregard and contempt for human rights have resulted in barbarous acts which have outraged the conscience of mankind; Whereas it is essential, if man is not to be compelled to have recourse, as a last resort, to rebellion against tyranny and oppression, that human rights should be protected by the rule of law; Whereas Member States have pledged themselves to achieve, in cooperation with the United Nations, the promotion of universal respect for and observance of human rights and fundamental freedoms; Whereas a common understanding of these rights and freedoms is of the greatest importance for the full realization of this pledge; Now, therefore, the General Assembly proclaims this Universal Declaration of Human Rights as a common standard of achievement for all peoples and all nations, to the end that every individual and every organ of society, keeping this Declaration constantly in mind, shall strive by teaching and education to promote respect for these rights and freedoms and by progressive measures, national and international, to secure their universal and effective recognition and observance, both among the peoples of Member States themselves and among the peoples of territories under their jurisdiction."

No wonder prohibitionists do not want to look at the problem with human rights. As society awakens from a collective psychosis, the ground beneath prohibitionists' feet gives way, and they are on the wrong side of the law. Even so, our obligations to human rights mean nothing if we deny this basic protection to drug law violators. Moral panic is detected, and we now must live with ourselves in the wee hours of the morning when society begins the process of restoration. There is no other way. The Preamble of the International Covenant on Civil and Political Rights emphasizes "the obligation of States under the Charter of the United Nations to promote universal respect for, and observance of, human rights and freedoms." It reaffirms "that these rights derive from the inherent dignity of the human person," and "that the individual, having duties to other individuals and to the community to which he belongs, is under a responsibility to strive for the promotion and observance of the rights recognized in the present Covenant." Furthermore, its article 3 holds that "The States Parties to the present Covenant undertake to ensure the equal right of men and women to the enjoyment of all civil and political rights set forth in the present Covenant"; its article 5 reiterates that "Nothing in the present Covenant may be interpreted as implying for any

State, group or person any right to engage in any activity or perform any act aimed at the destruction of any of the rights and freedoms recognized herein or at their limitation to a greater extent than is provided for in the present Covenant"; its article 14 reaffirms that "All persons shall be equal before the courts and tribunals. In the determination of any criminal charge against him, or of his rights and obligations in a suit at law, everyone shall be entitled to a fair and public hearing by a competent, independent and impartial tribunal established by law"; its article 16 repeats that "Everyone shall have the right to recognition everywhere as a person before the law"; its article 17 assures that "No one shall be subjected to arbitrary or unlawful interference with his privacy, family, home or correspondence, nor to unlawful attacks on his honor and reputation" and that "Everyone has the right to the protection of the law against such interference or attacks"; its article 26 emphasizes the absolute abrogation of discriminatory practices, declaring that "All persons are equal before the law and are entitled without any discrimination to the equal protection of the law. In this respect, the law shall prohibit any discrimination and guarantee to all persons equal and effective protection against discrimination on any ground such as race, color, sex, language, religion, political or other opinion, national or social origin, property, birth or other status"; its article 46 reiterates that "Nothing in the present Covenant shall be interpreted as impairing the provisions of the Charter of the United Nations"; and its article 47 reaffirms that "Nothing in the present Covenant shall be interpreted as impairing the inherent right of all peoples to enjoy and utilize fully and freely their natural wealth and resources."

All in all, then, there can be no doubt about the State's duty to promote, protect, and secure our rights. The Council of Europe, as well as UN agencies have provided guidelines to ensure that drug policy is compatible with this basic set up.[*] As the latter has to say on accountability and the right to an effective remedy:

*"Everyone has the right to an effective remedy in the event of actions and omissions that undermine or jeopardise their human rights, including where these actions or omissions relate to drug policy. In accordance with these rights, States should: (1) Establish appropriate, accessible, and effective legal, administrative, and other procedures to ensure the human rights compliant implementation of any law, policy, or practice related to drugs. (2) Ensure that independent and transparent legal mechanisms and procedures are available, accessible, and affordable for individuals and groups to make formal complaints about alleged human rights violations in the context of drug control laws, policies, and practices. (3) Ensure independent, impartial, prompt, and thorough investigations of allegations of human rights violations in the context of drug control laws, policies, and*

---

[*] COE, *Drug Policy and Human Rights: A Baseline Study* (2019) UNDP, UNAIDS, WHO, *International Guidelines on Human Rights and Drug Policy* (2020)

*practices. (4) Ensure that those responsible are held accountable for such violations in accordance with criminal, civil, administrative, or other law, as appropriate. (5) Ensure that adequate, appropriate, and effective remedies and means of redress are available, accessible, and affordable for all individuals and groups whose rights have been found to be violated as a result of drug control laws, policies, and practices. This should include accessible information on mechanisms and processes for seeking remedies and redress, and appropriate means of ensuring the timely enforcement of remedies. (6) Take effective measures to prevent the recurrence of human rights violations in the context of drug control laws, policies, and practices.*"[54]

Even so, despite this basis, prohibitionists at the UN, COE, and elsewhere, continue to shield the drug law from scrutiny. In books like *Constitutional Challenges to the Drug Law*, *Reason Is*, and *Human Rising*, I have shown how the European and American systems of law both have failed their populations. With a very few exceptions, every time a challenge against the drug law has been made, the system collapses at the state-level, and neither the European Court of Human Rights, the Council of Europe, or the UN Human Rights apparatus will intervene and recognize that this basic set up extends to drug prohibition.[*] Despite having received

---

[*] See correspondence of the Alliance for rights-oriented drug policies (AROD) with governments, national- and supranational agencies at www.arodpolicies.org/archive.

evidence of the drug laws' incompatibility with human rights; despite having seen that the destructive effects of prohibition (as well as its futility) is generally agreed upon; despite having seen that a majority of experts agree with the basic premises of the complaint; and despite having seen that professors of law agree with its legal reasoning, these institutions will not submit the drug law to review.

Hence, today, some 300 million drug users, having been denied an effective remedy, are without basic human rights protection. We are dealing with a crisis of law that is unparalleled in modern times. Millions of people are suffering arbitrary persecution and imprisonment. And now that we have established that *all laws* must conform to the test of legality, necessity, reasonableness, and legitimate purpose— and that *all people*, without distinction of any kind, are entitled to the rights and freedoms set forth in this Bill—we shall have more to say on the articles that undermine prohibition.[*]

# 4.1. Relevant articles of the UDHR and ICCPR

Drug prohibition is clashing with the Universal Declaration of Human Rights article 1, which holds that "All human beings are born free and equal in dignity and rights. They are

---

[*] We have already, in chapter 3, seen how the drug law is in violation of ICCPR article 26, so we shall not discuss it here.

endowed with reason and conscience and should act towards one another in a spirit of brotherhood." We are, after all, dealing with a discriminatory, disproportional, arbitrary, and profoundly unjust practice which every year kills around 300,000 people and wrongfully imprisons 10 million more. We would not subject anyone but drug law violators to such treatment; even if alcohol drinkers and obese people represent a much greater cost to society, we could not find legitimate reasons for persecuting a group as we do to the drug law violators, and so, obviously, all human beings are NOT born free and equal in dignity—and their persecution is not in the spirit of brotherhood.

Now, we have seen how drug prohibition destroys society, and as 33 countries have death penalties for drug law violations, we can say that it violates ICCPR article 6 which holds that "Every human being has the inherent right to life," and that "No one shall be arbitrarily deprived of his life." All these articles inform on each other, and as the system of prohibition represents a discriminatory and arbitrary practice, victims of prohibition are most certainly "arbitrarily deprived of their life."

The right to life is further mentioned in the Universal Declaration's article 3 and ICCPR article 9, which states that "Everyone has the right to life, liberty, and the security of person." The latter elaborates, adding that "No one shall be subjected to arbitrary arrest or detention," and that "No one shall be deprived of his liberty except on such grounds and in accordance with such procedure as are established by law." Now, "liberty of person" concerns freedom from confinement of the body, not a general freedom of action. Nonetheless, we fail to include the drug law violators, considering that they, having been denied the right to a fair trial and effective remedy, are fair game for the police state and arbitrarily being deprived of life, liberty, and the security of person.

Speaking of "arbitrary arrest and detention," the principle of proportionality is connected to the principle of arbitrariness. This means that if prohibitionists cannot defend the Status Quo, not only shall the drug laws be removed but millions of people currently imprisoned shall be released. This, of course, is difficult for prohibitionists to accept. Yet ICCPR article 9 prohibits arbitrary detention, and as the UN Working Group on Arbitrary Detention concludes: "[detention is arbitrary] when it is clearly impossible to invoke any legal basis justifying the deprivation of liberty" (category I) and "when the deprivation of liberty constitutes a violation of international law for reasons of discrimination . . . and which aims towards or can result in ignoring the equality of human rights" (category V).[55]

Its category II explicitly mentions violations of ICCPR article 26. And as the Human Rights Committee, in its General Comment no. 35, holds that "Arrest or detention on discriminatory grounds in violation of article 2, paragraph 1, article 3, or article 26 is in principle arbitrary", this issue is beyond serious dispute.

The reason is the connection between moral panic and human rights violations. To the extent that society is plagued by this phenomenon, segments of society will be persecuted for no good reason, and this is clearly the case. As shown in

*Human Rising*, only scapegoating and powerpolitics sustains the status quo. Thus, restoration becomes apparent. And while matters of restorative justice should be the focus of a truth and reconciliation commission, people are entitled to reparations for the horribles they have endured. Paragraph 5 of article 9 of the ICCPR provides that anyone who has been the victim of unlawful arrest or detention shall have an enforceable right to compensation, and in its General Comment no. 35 the Human Rights Committee elaborates:

> *"The State party remains responsible for adherence and ensuring adherence to article 9. It must rigorously limit those powers and must provide strict and effective control to ensure that those powers are not misused, and do not lead to arbitrary or unlawful arrest or detention. It must also provide effective remedies for victims if arbitrary or unlawful arrest or detention does occur."*

Defenders of the status quo may argue that only arrests lacking legal basis is arbitrary and that if there is a law—and the deprivation of liberty is done in accordance with such procedure as are established by law—everything is as it should be. This, however, is not so. As the Human Rights Committee says:

> *"An arrest or detention may be authorized by domestic law and nonetheless be arbitrary. The notion of 'arbitrariness' is not to be equated with 'against the*

*law,' but must be interpreted more broadly to include elements of inappropriateness, injustice, lack of predictability, and due process of law, as well as elements of reasonableness, necessity, and proportionality.* "[56]

Hence, currently some 10 million people are the victims of arbitrary detention, and the rule of law dictates that they shall be released and reimbursed for their hardships.

Let us not forget that article 9 also protects the "security of person." This is a broader concept than that of "liberty," which concerns freedom from confinement of the body. As interpreted by the Human Rights Committee, "Security of person concerns freedom from injury to the body and the mind, *or bodily and mental integrity*", and considering (1) that 80 percent of the 160,000 annual drug deaths can be attributed to prohibition;[57] considering (2) that 100 percent of the people who die as a result of the drugs economy must be credited to prohibition; considering (3) that prohibition generates many other types of crime and that the illegal economy corrupts democratic institutions and processes; considering (4) that the spraying of illegal crops destroys the livelihood of third world farmers, ruining foods, spreading death and disease among both livestock and people; considering (5) that the persecution of drug law violators not only defies their bodily and mental integrity, but damages the fabric of society, tearing families apart, spreading fear, prejudice, ignorance, death, and disease; and considering (6) that this summary only scratches the surface of the problems caused by prohibition, it is safe to say that we are dealing with a violation of the right to security of person.

The content of article 9 is informed by other articles. ICCPR article 7 and the Universal Declaration's article 5 holds that "No one shall be subjected to torture or to cruel, inhuman or degrading treatment or punishment." The aim of these provisions is to protect both the dignity and the physical and mental integrity of the individual. Whether we are dealing with "cruel, inhuman, or degrading treatment or punishment" depends on the nature, purpose, and severity of the treatment applied—and as we would not have accepted such treatment of alcohol drinkers or barkeepers, we are dealing with "inhuman or degrading treatment or punishment."

In addition to this, the Universal Declaration's article 12 and ICCPR article 17 holds that "No one shall be subjected to arbitrary interference with his privacy, family, home, or correspondence, nor to attacks upon his honor and reputation," and that "Everyone has the right to the protection of the law against such interference or attacks."

This article provides a right of every person to be protected against arbitrary or unlawful interference with his privacy. However, before we jump to conclusions on this section, let us look at the definition of "arbitrary" or "unlawful" interference. In its General Comment no. 16, the Human Rights Committee elaborates: "The term "unlawful" means that no interference can take place except in cases envisaged by the law. Interference authorized by States can only take place on the basis of law, *which itself must comply with the provisions, aims and objectives of the Covenant.*" As pertains to "arbitrary interference", it goes on to state: "in the Committee's view, the expression 'arbitrary interference" can also extend to interference provided for under the law. *The introduction of the concept of arbitrariness is intended to guarantee that even interference provided for by law should be in accordance with the provisions, aims and objectives of the Covenant and should be, in any event, reasonable in the particular circumstances.*"

Considering, therefore, that drug prohibition is shown to be a prejudiced and disproportional practice, the provisions of the UDHR article 12 and ICCPR article 17 protects against such interference.

Another article is the UDHR article 18 and ICCPR article 18 which affirms that "Everyone has the right to freedom of thought, conscience and religion; this right includes freedom . . . to manifest his religion or belief in teaching, practice, worship and observance." The latter goes further, adding that, "No one shall be subject to coercion which would impair his freedom to have or to adopt a religion or belief of his choice," and that "Freedom to manifest one's religion or beliefs may be subject only to such limitations as are prescribed by law and are necessary to protect public safety, order, health, or morals or the fundamental rights and freedoms of others."

Again, the proportionality principle comes into play. And in its General Comment no. 22 the Human Rights Committee expands on its implications:

*"Article 18 (3) permits restrictions on the freedom to manifest religion or belief only if limitations are*

*prescribed by law and are necessary to protect public safety, order, health or morals, or the fundamental rights and freedoms of others. . . . In interpreting the scope of permissible limitation clauses, States parties should proceed from the need to protect the rights guaranteed under the Covenant, including the right to equality and non-discrimination on all grounds specified in articles 2, 3 and 26. . . . Limitations may be applied only for those purposes for which they were prescribed and must be directly related and proportionate to the specific need on which they are predicated. Restrictions may not be imposed for discriminatory purposes or applied in a discriminatory manner. The Committee observes that the concept of morals derives from many social, philosophical and religious traditions; consequently, limitations on the freedom to manifest a religion or belief for the purpose of protecting morals must be based on principles not deriving exclusively from a single tradition."*

As we can see, even if the religious use of psychedelic substances may be unheard of, principles of proportionality and equality come into play when rulers prohibit religious practices they themselves do not understand. And as the drug law, as measured against the test of reason, have been weighed and found wanting, it does not look good for prohibitionists.

Of course, this argument presumes that drugs can be useful, that they can connect us with the divine, and be of use in a spiritual endeavor. To a prohibitionist this may seem far-fetched, but there is a wealth of material that attests to such use. Indeed, psychoactive substances like cannabis, peyote, mescaline, ayahuasca, ibogaine, and psilocybin-containing mushrooms have been used for millennia by people who claim that these drugs can help us experience divinity more directly—and despite efforts to eradicate such use, it is more widespread than ever. While much use is private, there are religious communities with a license to use these substances. In the United States, the *Native American Church* has a membership of 250,000 people who use mescaline-containing cactus to communicate with spirit. In Latin America, there is the *Santo Daime* and the *União do Vegetal* who use a DMT-containing brew called ayahuasca for similar purposes; and in West Africa, we have the Bwiti who use ibogaine.

Prohibitionists may dismiss such activities, thinking drugs and religion to be separate realms, qualitatively miles apart. Nonetheless, studies support the contentions of drug users, and the fact that even the US Supreme Court has recognized such use as legit speaks volumes. After all, the evidence is frowned upon by prohibitionists in power, and had they found a way to discredit religious use, they would. We shall not elaborate on the many[58] scientific reports on psychedelics, nor the abundance of books that detail the use of drugs as a gateway to enlightenment and communion with the Divine. Suffice to say that it is well documented. For this reason, research into psychedelics has been revived, and a solid case can be made that drug prohibition is incompatible with our right to religion.

While we are at it, we must investigate if prohibition is compatible with the other provisions of article 18. After all, this article does not only recognize a freedom of religion; it recognizes a freedom of thought and conscience, and this is far-reaching and profound. This article encompasses freedom of thought on all matters pertaining to personal conviction, whether manifested individually or in community with others. The fundamental character of this freedom is mirrored in the fact that this provision cannot be derogated from even in time of public emergency, as stated in article 4 (2) of the Covenant. It does not permit *any limitations whatsoever* on the freedom of thought and conscience, or on the freedom to have or adopt a religion or belief of one's choice.

The fundamental status of a freedom of thought is important because drugs offer an opportunity to see the world from a new perspective. Prohibitionists have a problem accepting this, but brilliant minds can testify that drug use has helped shape their vision. Nobel Laureates have admitted as much, and Kary Mullins, a chemist who won the Nobel Prize in 1993, stated that "I think I might have been stupid in some respects if it weren't for my psychedelic experiences."[59]

There are studies that attest to the same, and to prohibit drug use is an infringement on our freedom of thought. Such a freedom, after all, must include a freedom to choose cognitive processes, to select how to feel, and to control one's own thinking processes, for as Thomas B. Roberts, a professor of educational psychology at Northern Illinois University, stated:

*"Our thinking is composed of both (1) the way we think (the cognitive processes we use and our skills in using them) and (2) the specific content of our thoughts (our*

This should be obvious. After all, what good is a freedom of thought that does not recognize the right to independent thinking, to autonomy over our own mind and brain chemistry, and the right to experience the full spectrum of possible thought and consciousness?

While the Bill of Rights fails to enumerate an absolute freedom of cognition, it is implicit in the spirit of the doctrine, as it is a basis for enumerated rights. If a freedom of thought is to mean anything, therefore, it must include the freedom to stimulate the mind. And this, as lawyer Allison Brandi Margolin asserts, includes "the freedom to explore one's mind, to do something to create a thought that would not otherwise be created without the antecedent action, e.g., taking drugs."[61]

The reason why this has not been self-evident is that prohibitionists believe that there is only one correct way of thinking—theirs. However, as psychology have evolved, we have learned to recognize that there are higher, more advanced states of consciousness. These are referred to as "unitive states of consciousness," and while they can be reached by other methods, psychoactive drugs are trustworthy tools. They have an ability to expand the ego-consciousness into greater territories of the psyche. Thus, they make it possible to become acquainted with unrecognized aspects of our psyche—and when we have worked through our issues and transcended old and erroneous beliefs, a higher state of consciousness is achieved.

Research shows that people who have experienced this shift of consciousness tend to be better educated, more successful, more responsible, more confident, less racist, and happier on measures of psychological well-being. They are less attached to materialistic possessions; they have greater ego-strength; they live more meaningful lives; they are less afraid of death and hardships; they are more imaginative, self-sufficient, intelligent, and relaxed.[62]

The empirical data is overwhelming. Since prohibition began, there has been a cognitive revolution which recognizes a new, multistate perspective on our minds. This cognitive revolution has not yet been acknowledged by prohibitionists, and it is time that they recognize the fallacy of the single-state theory. As a matter of fact, prohibition has slowed the progress of science. Researchers in the 1950-60s were only beginning to understand the potential of psychoactive drugs when lawmakers put an end to a promising era of research. Despite the hurdles put in place by prohibition, however, scientists have gathered evidence that validates the expanded states of consciousness as well as the potential of psychedelic drugs for human evolution.

From what has been said, we can also see how prohibition is in violation of UDHR article 19 and ICCPR article 19. The former holds that "Everyone has the right to freedom of opinion and expression; this right includes freedom to hold opinions without interference and to seek, receive, and impart information and ideas through any media and regardless of frontiers." The latter elaborates on these provisions. Its paragraph 1 concerns the freedom to hold opinions, while paragraph 2 deals with the freedom of expression, adding that "this right shall include freedom to seek, receive, and impart information and ideas of all kinds, regardless of frontiers, either orally, in writing or in print, in the form of art, or through any other media of his choice."

While the freedom of opinion is absolute, the freedom of expression is more restricted. Its paragraph 3 elaborates: "The exercise of the rights provided for in paragraph 2 of this article carries with it special duties and responsibilities. It may therefore be subject to certain restrictions, but these shall only be such as are provided by law and are necessary: (a) For respect of the rights or reputations of others; (b) For the protection of national security or of public order, or of public health or morals."

This freedom of opinion and expression forms a basis for the enjoyment of many other human rights and is closely related to the previously discussed article 18. In its General Comment no. 34, the Human Rights Committee elaborates: "Freedom of opinion and freedom of expression are indispensable conditions for the full development of the person. They are essential for any society. They constitute the foundation stone for every free and democratic society. The two freedoms are closely related, with freedom of expression providing the vehicle for the exchange and development of opinions." To emphasize the importance of a freedom of expression, the Committee goes on to note:

> *"The concept of morals derives from many social, philosophical and religious traditions; consequently, limitations for the purpose of protecting morals must be based on principles not deriving exclusively from a single tradition. Any such limitations must be understood in the light of universality of human rights and the principle of non-discrimination. . . . The scope of paragraph 2 embraces even expression that may be regarded as deeply offensive."*

The proportionality principle coming into play, the State must demonstrate the legal basis for any restrictions. It must demonstrate in specific fashion the precise nature of the threat; it must demonstrate that the restriction is necessary and has a legitimate purpose (i.e., it must be appropriate to achieve its protective function) and that the restriction is not overbroad (i.e., it must be the least intrusive instrument amongst those which might achieve a protective function). As the Committee continues in General Comment 34:

> *"When a State party invokes a legitimate ground for restriction of freedom of expression, it must demonstrate in specific and individualized fashion the*

*precise nature of the threat, and the necessity and proportionality of the specific action taken, in particular by establishing a direct and immediate connection between the expression and the threat."*

Now, the drug law has proved to be a worse malady than drug use, and so the State will have difficulty in convincing an independent, impartial, and competent commission of the necessity of a restriction on our freedom of expression. After all, there can be no doubt that "the right to seek, receive, and impart information and ideas of all kinds regardless of frontiers" includes the right to explore the expanded states of consciousness, and as psychoactive drugs are needed for most to arrive at these levels of consciousness, prohibition is incompatible with the provisions of this article.

Continuing to the next set of articles, the Universal Declaration's article 20 and ICCPR article 20 holds that "Any propaganda for war shall be prohibited by law," and that "any advocacy of national, racial, or religious hatred that constitutes incitement to discrimination, hostility, or violence shall be prohibited by law."

Connecting this article to prohibition is simple. But before we point out the obvious, let us see what the Human Rights Committee has to say on this article:

*"The prohibition under paragraph 1 extends to all forms of propaganda threatening or resulting in an act of aggression or breach of the peace contrary to the Charter of the United Nations, while paragraph 2 is*

This article applies to prohibition because the war on drugs has been a war on truth. The idea of prohibition as a decent endeavor begins with us first accepting the enemy image of drugs, and only to the degree this perceived threat is allowed to grow in our minds will we accept its premises. If it were not for the moral panic that follows in the wake of this enemy image, we would have understood that drug users have the same rights as anyone else to be protected against discriminatory, disproportionate, and arbitrary practices. We would have seen through the prejudice and misconceptions that govern prohibitionist reasoning, and we would not have accepted the senseless persecution of drug law violators.

However, so it is. For more than 50 years, we have been blind to the detrimental effects of prohibition; we have been so afraid that we have accepted the worst transgressions, and all because of a greatly exaggerated enemy image.

Now, the only way that evidence-based drug policies and rational debate could be held at bay was by the prohibitionists taking control of the debate. Truth being their enemy, they had to rely on propaganda to make themselves look good. They had to create a moral climate where they held the high-ground and where anyone opposing their policies was a suspect. They had to advocate a system of thought where no objections were allowed, where they had a monopoly on the truth, and where people blindly submitted to totalitarian premises. Only in such a world could their ideology thrive—and to the extent that it has prevailed, it is because of such conditions.

Hence, the war on drugs could never have gained ground without a massive propaganda apparatus at the prohibitionists' disposal. Since day one, it was evident for those with eyes to see that prohibition was brought into being by a corrupt political process; that it, as Judge James P. Gray noted, was "motivated by racism, fear, empire building, and ignorance"[64]; that prohibitionists distorted or disregarded the evidence to have their way[65], and that voices of reason were censored[66] or ignored. Thanks to the propaganda apparatus, however, prohibition has continued to this day supported by an unbroken chain of self-serving bureaucrats,[67] even though it has been evident all along that an unbiased analysis, whether by cost-benefit[68] or human rights criteria,[69] would favor a regulation of drugs.

The propaganda for war has been so complete that the masses have been enthralled. It has inflicted a state of collective psychosis where it has been impossible to those caught in its grip to put two and two together. The navel-gazing and denial of reality is proof of this: prohibitionists have so much prestige, so much power, so much money invested in this ride that they have set aside the rule of law rather than let reality hamper their delusion. Hence, we are here, where 300 million people are without the protection of human rights while prohibitionists continue their persecution with no shame.

We have already seen why almost 100 years of warfare ensure that this regime can be classified as a crime against humanity. Because of this war, we have a state apparatus dedicated to making life a living hell for drug law violators; because of this war, several millions have died while hundreds of millions have been thrown in prison; because of this war, the United States (adjusted for population) enslaves about 6 times as many black citizens as South Africa did under apartheid; and because of this war, 25 percent of African-Americans who grew up in the past three decades have had at least one parent locked up during their childhood.[70]

All being connected, we see from this how families are destroyed by the drug war. Hence, prohibition is in violation of ICCPR article 23, which states that "The family is the natural and fundamental group unit of society and is entitled to protection by society and the State."

*None of this* would have been possible without the propaganda apparatus. Ignorance and arrogance alone have contributed to this parade of horribles and knowing that the persecution of drug users represents a discriminatory and disproportional practice, we are dealing with a violation of article 20.

# 5

# The Right to a Fair Trial and Effective Remedy

*"It is for you to realize these rights, now and for all time. Human rights are your rights. Seize them. Defend them. Promote them. Understand them and insist on them. Nourish and enrich them!"*

*—Kofi Annan, UN Secretary General—*

WE HAVE SEEN how drug prohibition is in violation of ICCPR articles 2 (1), 2 (3a), 2 (3b), 5 (1), 5 (2), 6 (1), 7, 9 (1), 9 (5), 14 (1), 16, 17 (1), 17 (2), 18 (1), 18 (3), 19 (2), 19 (3), 20 (1), 20 (2), 23 (1), 26, 46 and 47, as well as the Universal Declaration's articles 1, 2, 3, 5, 6, 7, 8, 9, 10, 12, 18, 19, 28, 29 (1), 29 (2), 29 (3) and 30. They all touch upon problematic aspects of the status quo, and now that we have seen how drug policy is incompatible with human rights principles, we shall discuss the possibilities for effecting change.

There are several ways to do this. The easiest (at least, the least stressful) is discussing it with others, writing about it in the media, or informing politicians of the relationship between human rights and drug prohibition. If you choose the latter, politicians will have a duty to assist in having the issue reviewed, and they can be held liable for aiding and abetting in crimes against humanity if they fail to do so. As seen, the human rights conventions declare that public officials have a positive obligation to take allegations of human rights violations seriously and provide standards against which state actors can be held accountable. Having received evidence that indicates a violation of human rights, they are required to act, and so this is a way forward.

What I recommend, therefore, is to write to politicians, present them with information suggestive of the drug laws' incompatibility with human rights, and ask that (1) a national commission is set up, one that independently, impartially, and competently can have the issue reviewed; and (2), considering that drug prohibition is a worldwide problem, organized from the UN level, that they work to have the issue resolved internationally. The UN General Assembly have special sessions on drugs, and officials should ensure that the rights-oriented debate gets the attention it deserves.

As the failures of prohibition are becoming more evident, there has been a movement towards change. Human rights have begun to influence the debate, but state actors still shy away from meaningful analysis. Even so, while principled perspectives are for the future to behold, it need not be long. Canada and other nations already point to the Convention on the rights of the Child to justify a regulation of cannabis. Prohibitionists, for their part, claim that this is in breach of UN drug control obligations, and so the time has come to investigate what regime is in violation of the human rights conventions.

To specify the essence of the rights-oriented debate, there are four questions that must be answered to the satisfaction of an impartial, independent, and competent tribunal for drug prohibition to be found compatible with our Bill of Rights. Provided that our leaders recognize the rights-oriented debate, these questions can, using cannabis as an example, be stated like this:

• Whereas comparisons of the problems associated with cannabis and legal drugs like alcohol and tobacco[71] demonstrate that the legal ones are more harmful to health and more destructive to society: *How can drug policy be defended? How can prohibitionists, without building policy on a discriminatory practice— and thus violate the principle of equality—argue in favor of a health-oriented approach towards alcohol users and a continued criminalization of cannabis users?*

• Whereas there is the same law of supply and demand when it comes to cannabis and alcohol and tobacco, and whereas the different groups of drugs also have the same varying patterns of use:[72] *How will prohibitionists justify the persecution and the demonization of drug law violators? What crimes against his fellowmen has a cannabis producer, transporter, or seller committed that an alcohol producer, transporter, or seller has not done?*

• Whereas the world's leading drug policy scholars are in agreement that the drug laws have had worse consequences for society in general and users in particular than the drug use,[73] and whereas more and more organizations and commissions[74] publish reports confirming the same: *How will prohibitionists, from the growing evidence base that suggests that the cure (cannabis prohibition) is worse than the disease (cannabis use) defend current policy as measured against the principle of proportionality?*

• Whereas drug policy scholars agree that there was a moral panic behind the outlawing of cannabis;[75] whereas professionals acknowledge that its current classification makes no sense;[76] whereas scholarly works such as James Ostrowski's *Answering the Critics of Drug Legalization*, Douglas Husak's *Drugs and Rights*, and David A.J. Richards' *Sex, Drugs, Death, and the Law* have refuted the arguments in favor of criminalization; whereas an independent, impartial, and competent tribunal (the Cannabis-tribunal in the Hague, 2008) has qualified the prohibitionist argument as "based on fallacies" and "absolutely worthless,"[77] whereas constitutional courts in Mexico, South Africa, Alaska, and Georgia have concluded the same; whereas the drug law thus seem to build on a series of faulty premises: Considering that the enemy image of cannabis has proven vastly exaggerated; considering that the separation between licit and illicit substances has proven an arbitrary divide; considering that that the evidence is clear that the drug laws have failed to reduce the supply and demand:[78] considering that American, as well as European[79] decriminalization experiments have shown a health-oriented approach to be more successful in dealing with the harms caused by drug use;[80] considering that the cure has proven worse than the disease to the point where the harms associated with prohibition[81] threaten to undermine the very fabric of our society;[82] considering that paternalistic and moralistic arguments have failed and considering that prohibitionists can no longer justify policy on the basis that (1) it suppresses different types of crime,[83] (2) that it protects youth[84] and society,[85] (3) that drug abuse has substantial economic and social costs,[86] (4) that cannabis use is intrinsically immoral[87] and degrading, (5) that its use is self-destructive, dangerous, and may cause a variety of harms, including physical injury, addiction, and death,[88] (6) that it is a gateway drug,[89] (7) that its use is not a victimless crime,[90] and (8) that we do not know the consequences of legalization:[91] *All this considered, what compelling reasons can there be for prohibition, and how are its means tailored towards its explicitly stated ends?*

Cannabis has been used as an example because the evidence is compelling. Thus, if prohibitionists cannot answer these questions—and they recognize that the Bill of Rights protects *all people* against disproportionate, arbitrary, and discriminatory intrusions and that the test of reason applies to the drug law—we can agree that current policy presents a grave violation of human rights.

To prohibitionists, there is no way out of this predicament. To justify the status quo, they must convince an independent, impartial, and competent tribunal. The only way to avoid this would be to deny the merits of the rights-oriented debate all together. And if prohibitionists, suspecting that they cannot refute these questions, should continue to deny human rights protection to the persecuted groups, they must invalidate this chain of reasoning and confront the following question:

• Whereas there is a fundamental principle of our system of law that the individual is to have as much freedom, responsibility, and self-determination as is possible (that is, as compatible with a similar right and freedom of others); whereas weighty societal considerations must necessitate such actions if our rights and freedoms shall be restricted (i.e., restrictions must be required for the protection of the general welfare and the purpose of securing due recognition and respect for the rights and freedoms of others); whereas the purpose of human rights law is to ensure that this is so and to protect the individual from undue, unjust, and arbitrary interferences; whereas at the core of the Bill of Rights therefore we find a code of ethics, principles that are derived from the Wholeness, mirrored in all humanitarian values, and that bring together constitutional law, social contractarian thought and moral theory; whereas the articles of the Bill of Rights are the result of these principles and established to promote them so that we mature towards greater levels of understanding; whereas the Bill of Rights is established  to ensure to all people, *without distinction of any kind*, protection against discriminatory, unjust, and disproportional practices; whereas this includes the world's 200-300 million drug users, and whereas the objective of human rights law therefore is to secure *also to them* the rights and protections recognized in the Bill of Rights: Considering that public officials undertake to strive for the advancement and observance of the rights and protections recognized in this Bill; considering that the principles they have a duty to promote and protect establish criteria that our system of law must honor to be lawful; considering that drug reform activists have assembled irresistible evidence that the drug laws, as measured against these criteria, are found wanting; considering that these laws have been so destructive that they fulfill the criteria as gross human rights violations and crimes against humanity; considering that activists have presented documentation and that legal scholars and drug policy experts have concluded the same; considering that former UN Secretary Generals and High Commissioners for Human Rights have attested to this factual picture; considering that you have been presented with four questions that must be answered to the satisfaction of an independent, impartial, and competent tribunal if these scholars' and experts' conclusions are to be refuted; considering that the prohibitionist regime has never been submitted to the test of reason and that our officials have refused to respond to these questions; considering that *the rule of law demands that they be answered*, but that every official confronted with the matter has flouted his duties and denied an effective remedy; considering that 300 million drug users therefore are without the protection of human rights, and considering that the validity of the social contract and the credibility of civil servants depends on taking the promotion and observance of human rights law seriously; considering that public officials have a responsibility not only to drug users, but humanity and the rule of law; considering that, objectively speaking, the legalization argument is fair and that to protect the integrity of the Bill of Rights, officials need to ensure that human rights rule supreme, that the matter is reviewed, and that questions are satisfactorily answered; considering that if our officials fail to do so without adequately addressing the issues raised herein—that is, explaining *wherein* this chain of reasoning officials disagree and/or *what more* corroboration is needed to substantiate contentions—it will become evident that opposition to drug reform is blind; that it is motivated by ignorance and ignoble ambitions, and that civil servants are abusing authority in an attempt to arrest the development of human rights; considering that, in doing so, public officials are proven enemies of humanity, standing with war profiteers and gangsters against the rule of law and the human race, and that they can be persecuted as participants in crimes against humanity: *All this considered, how can prohibitionists maintain that the principles of human rights do not apply to the drug law? How will you explain your position and your rationale that drug users are exempt from a catalogue of rights that is inherent to every human being?*

This is the great challenge. Only in answering these questions can prohibitionists stand their ground; only in doing so can they ensure that drug policy is compatible with the Bill of Rights; only in doing so can they assure drug users that rights are respected; and only in doing so can the State adhere to the rule of law.

In theory, therefore, getting politicians to answer these questions and to provide an effective remedy should be straightforward. In practice, however, it is not that simple. Organizations like the Alliance for rightsoriented drug policies (AROD) have presented this documentation more than 500 times to Norwegian officials and none have cared. For some reason, they are committed to ignorance, and COE-, UN-, and

US officials have also spaced out into an incoherent state of mind when confronted with the facts.

This, of course, will not relieve them of responsibility. The evidence is in and we are dealing with a crime against humanity. A failure to provide an effective remedy, at this stage, only means that nations have a responsibility to deal with such officials at a later stage. For now, however, theory and practice are different worlds, and it is up to us to bridge this gap.

When it comes to this, we are uniquely positioned. As a starter, talking with friends and colleagues makes sense. Some may want to become activists, demonstrating in the streets or writing to politicians to demand that human rights are taken seriously. Others may want to use the justice system to effect change. All non-violent options are on the table. When dealing with gross violations of human rights, citizens are free to fight against the machine that has become an enemy of humanity. People are under no obligation to accept a social contract based on lies, exploitation, and injustice, and as the political machinery's force of inertia continues to ensure more crimes against humanity, we would do well to remember Mario Savo. As this activist of freedom cried out in his impassioned 1964-speech at Berkeley:

*"There comes a time when the operation of the machine becomes so odious, makes you so sick at heart, that you can't take part, you can't even tacitly take part, and you've got to put your bodies on the gears and upon the wheels, upon the levers, upon all the apparatus, and*

Now, the following is not for everyone. Still, a way forward is through the justice system. As seen in chapter one, our system is built on principles of law, and we can use the justice system to have rights recognized.

To understand how this works, it is useful to backtrack. In chapter one, we discussed principles of popular sovereignty and a separation of powers. The former states that all power emanates from the people. The government is to ensure that individual rights are respected, while the separation of powers is to ensure that factions are contained.

However, despite an independent press, special interests can become sufficiently powerful to subvert the political process—and here, the judiciary comes into play. As we have seen, the executive and the legislative branches of government have shied away from human rights responsibility and the judiciary has the power to correct this situation.

What people can do therefore, if caught violating the drug law, is to refuse to accept the law because it is a violation of human rights. The signatories to the human rights conventions have outlawed arbitrary, discriminatory, and disproportional practices. Thus, if a defendant declares that the drug law is precisely this kind of practice, the judge must grant the creation of an independent, impartial, and competent tribunal where the issue can be carefully reviewed.

The right to a fair trial and judicial review is detailed in the human rights conventions (such as ECHR articles 6 and 13 and ICCPR articles 2 and 14). In chapter four, we saw articles in the UN Bill of Rights which protected this right, and it is elaborated on in the Human Rights Committee's General Comments no. 31 and 32. In the former's paragraph 15, the Committee expands on State obligations:

> *"Article 2, paragraph 3, requires that in addition to effective protection of Covenant rights States Parties must ensure that individuals also have accessible and effective remedies to vindicate those rights. Such remedies should be appropriately adapted so as to take account of the special vulnerability of certain categories of person . . .*
>
> *The Committee attaches importance to States Parties' establishing appropriate judicial and administrative mechanisms for addressing claims of rights violations under domestic law . . . Administrative mechanisms are particularly required to give effect to the general obligation to investigate allegations of violations promptly, thoroughly, and effectively through independent and impartial bodies. . . . A failure by a State Party to investigate allegations of violations could in and of itself give rise to a separate breach of the Covenant. Cessation of an ongoing violation is an essential element of the right to an effective remedy."*

A judge is required to recognize our right to an effective remedy if we present documentation to support our charges.[*] This is a key to effecting human rights commitments, and in its General Comment no. 32, the Committee has more to say:

*"The notion of fair trial includes the guarantee of a fair and public hearing. Fairness of proceedings entails the absence of any direct or indirect influence, pressure or intimidation or intrusion from whatever side and for whatever motive. . . . Deviating from fundamental principles of fair trial . . . is prohibited at all times.*

*. . .The right to equality before courts and tribunals, in general terms, guarantees, in addition to the principles mentioned in the second sentence of Article 14, paragraph 1 [that everyone shall be entitled to a fair and public hearing by a competent, independent, and impartial tribunal established by law], those of equal access and equality of arms, and ensures that the parties to the proceedings in question are treated without any discrimination.*

*. . . The requirement of competence, independence, and impartiality of a tribunal in the sense of article 14, paragraph 1, is an absolute right that is not subject to any exception. . . . The requirement of impartiality has two aspects. First, judges must not allow their judgment to be influenced by personal bias or prejudice, nor*

---

[*] As a defence against drug prohibition, the Alliance for rightsoriented drug policies (AROD) recommends MIKALSEN, *HUMAN RISING* (2021). For Americans, MIKALSEN, *TO RIGHT A WRONG* (2021) should do.

*harbor preconceptions about the particular case before them, nor act in ways that improperly promote the interests of one of the parties to the detriment of the other. Second, the tribunal must also appear to a reasonable observer to be impartial."*

This is the essence of our right to a fair trial. And if the State fails to show that the drug law is necessary in a democratic society, it must be removed and the persecuted are entitled to compensation.[92]

It goes without saying that this is difficult for most to ponder. Moral panic has that effect. But for prohibitionists, what is even more disturbing is the responsibility of the State to ensure human rights violations are brought to justice.

This is imperative because strengthening accountability is key to human rights protection. Historically, a culture of impunity has been the greatest threat to the advancement of human rights, and the UN Human Rights Committee has noted that a "failure to bring to justice perpetrators of such violations could in and of itself give rise to a separate breach of the Covenant. . . . The States Parties concerned may not relieve perpetrators from personal responsibility . . . [and] no official status justifies persons who may be accused of responsibility for such violations being held immune from legal responsibility."[93]

In theory, we see that the right to a fair trial and effective remedy is at the heart of our justice system. It is so important that Johs. Andenæs, Norway's most renowned jurist, rated it top among the West's contributions to World civilization and he was not exaggerating. Our right to challenge the law is the safety valve when all else fails. It is a solution to the problem of arbitrary government—and if the State denies this right, its representatives have robbed us of our most effective defense against the police state.

It follows that if the State aspires to protect the rule of law and its own reputation officials must provide an effective remedy. And so, if persecuted for violating the drug law, it makes sense to put this wheel into motion.

The law, after all, is clear: (1) The principles of human rights provide values that is to guide governments; (2) it is plain to see that the drug law, as measured against these values and principles, is weighed and found wanting; and (3) there can be no doubt that the purpose of the Bill of Rights—and the rule of law—is to bridge the gap between human rights principles and their implementation. As signatories to the European Convention on Human Rights, European nations must adhere by these rules. As pertains to the world community, States have pledged allegiance to the principles of human rights with the UN Charter. As signatories to the International Covenant on Civil and Political Rights, they have a contractual obligation to protect and promote human rights, and as members of the United Nations they shall be dedicated to the continuous process of articulating human rights in order to translate them from morality and principles into binding international law.

Hence, no matter how much power, money, and prestige our officials have vested in prohibition, the gig is up. Moral panic has been detected, and officials have a duty to ensure that the drug law is submitted to the test of reason. While the European Court of Human Rights has shirked its assignments on this issue, the Pompidou Group and the Parliamentary Assembly have noted its aloofness with regret. The latter did a baseline report on human rights and drug policy to remedy the lack of communication on this issue, and the UN is no better. Its human rights apparatus has been informed for more than a decade on the problem of arbitrary persecution, but to no avail. Our human rights institutions will talk of human rights values, while they act as gatekeepers against meaningful change.

Still, more and more constitutional courts are doing things right, and it is becoming increasingly difficult to ignore the gap between prohibition and human rights obligations. The UN Human Rights Committee is clear that the Bill of Rights is to be a living instrument, flexible enough to protect the individual against all discriminatory, disproportionate, and arbitrary practices, and that addressing inequalities requires a focus on the marginalized and vulnerable. This makes it difficult to argue that drug users are exempt from a catalogue of rights that is inherent to every human person, and it is only a matter of time before the rights-oriented debate gets the attention it deserves.

It will not be long. As the consequences of prohibition become more palpable, people see beyond the lies, prejudices, and misconceptions that sustain drug policy. Prohibitionists can no longer limit real debate by claiming the moral high-ground and refusing to answer their critics. A century of prohibition policy has disproven key premises and setting aside the rule of law to shield the drug law from review is just making it worse.

The rights-oriented debate, most certainly, will not go away. No policy can survive supported by ignorance and arrogance alone. History is a testimony to our progression, and as humanity evolves, we break free from shackles of oppression. This is why lawyers have a saying. They know that the "law works itself pure", and that the spirit of freedom will always endure, much due to the inherent blueprint of divine law.

Hence, the fate of prohibition has been sealed since day one. It was never a matter of *if* this policy would end; it was only a matter of *when,* and the rights-oriented debate is sure to bring victory. The prohibitionists have no say. They can only accept the inevitable or display an ever more farcical contempt for the rule of law. Choosing to continue their denial of reality, however, will only add fuel to the fire, and so the endgame draws near.

In the final analysis, it depends on two variables: (1) how far prohibitionists will go to see justice denied, and (2) how much longer people will put up with self-serving civil servants who think they are above the law. When it comes to this, we cannot expect prohibitionists to abdicate power willingly. Power never does, and looking at history, rights are never given; they are always hard won, and while authorities, from time to time, have had to give a little in order not to lose everything, only human rights defenders of the past have kept tyranny in check. Thanks to them, we have our Bill of Rights, and it is up to us to ensure that rights are respected.

The state apparatus, after all, is never short on officials eager to thin out our catalogue of rights. They are constantly trying to increase the State's influence by diminishing ours, and if the public remains too complacent and apathetic to care, they will succeed. We see from this that there is a strong correlation between freedom and responsibility. In the end, only those worthy of liberty will retain it, and those who want freedom must be prepared to fight tyranny inch by inch.

In saying so, I am not advocating violent means. Only a non-violent revolution will be worthy of our cause, and freedom fighters will follow former champions of liberty such as Martin Luther King and Mahatma Gandhi. As these people have shown, the most effective tool against any form of tyranny is civil disobedience, but it must come from a place of love and not contempt. This is important, as the latter will increase hostilities, and this is not what we want. Any action, therefore, whether it is civil disobedience or merely discussing the issue with prohibitionists, should be inspired by love for humanity. If we want a better world, we must be the change we want to see, and to the extent that we build on first principles, the world will move forward.

Truth is, we will always get the kind of government we deserve. For those with eyes to see, public officials have nourished our capacity for scapegoating, and the only reason why this war could have lasted so long is because we were too timid to take responsibility for our own lives. In the name of the war on drugs, we have let the State take away our freedoms and our politicians' hypocrisy, short-sightedness, and lack of respect for human rights has mirrored our own.

Conversely, if we wise up, a more constructive dynamic will take place between the individual and the State: to the extent that we clean up our act, we will have civil servants who know their place within a framework of constructive social engineering; their motivation will be to serve rather than to suppress; they will not be corrupted by special interests, and they will have no need to empower themselves at our expense. Instead, the founders' principled thinking and its implications will be embedded in their reasoning and this will bridge the gap between theory and practice. Consequently, a new class of politicians will arise who will want to encourage individuality rather than suppress it; who will inspire us rather than disempower; and who will promote a sense of responsibility among the citizenry rather than discourage it.

Knowing this, people should be inspired to fight tyrannical government. As Field Marshal Ferdinand Foch once wrote "The most powerful weapon on earth is the human soul on fire," and truth being on our side, we cannot lose. Hence, a storm is brewing that will give rise to another chapter of human civilization. It will be an era of constructive social engineering, and those who have the courage are welcome on the barricades.

This is where the action is. This is where service to humanity is needed as we do have a say in the creation of our own reality. From a perspective of social engineering, there is only love and fear, and while the former is the engine of utopian society-building, the latter is the generator of Orwellian societies. Therefore, from the perspective of a constitutional scholar, we must choose between autonomy or tyranny, consciousness or unconsciousness, the rule of law or wanton persecution. There will be one or the other, and so the way forward should be straightforward. We all have an interest in ending the war on drugs, and it is as simple as two plus two: The more people demand answers, the harder it will be to ignore us; and the harder it becomes to ignore us, the sooner we will rid the world of a war that has trampled human rights, corrupted our thinking, and nearly destroyed a civilization.

# About the author

Roar Mikalsen is the author of six books which are changing the world one at a time. His authorship covers a large area ranging from cosmology, mysticism, self-help, and consciousness research to power politics, human rights law, drug policy, constitutional interpretation, and social engineering. He is the founder of the Alliance for Rights-Oriented Drug Policies (AROD), an organization which addresses drug policy reform from a perspective of human rights and a nominee of two prestigious human rights awards (Vaclav Havel and Martin Ennals).

A platform for his work is Life Liberty Productions, a publishing house and consulting agency dedicated to the Spirit of Freedom. You will find books that are embraced by professionals and have the potential to bring humanity one step further on the online store lifelibertybooks.com

# ENDNOTES

[1] Randy Barnett, a professor of law, commented: "It seems that no facts are sufficient to shake the prohibitionists' faith in this tragic policy. As . . . suggested elsewhere, some persons act as though they are addicted to drug laws, with all the connotations of irrationality that term is meant to convey when applied to drug users. Consequently, they are unlikely to be swayed by the copious facts and arguments presented [by reform activists]. . . . [Nonetheless] the case against prohibition is overwhelming, precisely because so many different types of considerations all point to a single solution: the legalization of illicit drugs." Randy E. Barnett, *Bad Trip: Drug Prohibition and the Weakness of Public Policy*, 103 Yale Law Journal (1994), p. 2598.

Drug war bureaucrats, however, have refused to acknowledge any of this, and for more on "the extent to which these hardliners have gone to maintain the status quo through rhetoric, denial, manipulation, selective presentation, misrepresentation and suppression of evidence, selective use of experts, threats to funding, and purging ''defeatists'' from the UN system", see Martin Jelsma, *Drugs in the UN System: the Unwritten History of the 1998 United Nations General Assembly Special Session on Drugs*, International Journal of Drug Policy 14 (2003), pp. 181-195; Francisco Thoumi & Jorrit Kamminga, *The Recent Changes at UNODC and its Role in Advancing and Innovating Anti-Drug Policies: Old Wine in New Cleaner Bottles;* Christopher Hallam, Dave Bewley-Taylor & Martin Jelsma, *Scheduling in the International Drug Control System*, Series on Legislative Reform of Drug Policies No. 25, TNI IDPC (June 2014).

Professors Bakalar and Grinspoon has this to say on the evolution of drug policy: "Looked at as a series of incidents, the history of social and legal responses to drug use, especially in the last century and in the United States, sometimes seems melancholy and haphazard. It is easy to find inadequate pharmacology, inconsistent ad hoc responses based on poor information, indulgence of passions and prejudices, including racism, in response to drug scares, institutional self-aggrandizement by narcotics police, and a fair amount of hypocrisy and corruption." JAMES B. BAKALAR & LESTER GRINSPOON, *DRUG CONTROL IN A FREE SOCIETY*, Cambridge University Press (1998), p. 68. For more on how prohibitionists have ignored the evidence, see infra notes 3, 14, 64, 65, 66, 74.

[2] John F. Galliher, David P. Keys & Michael Elsner, *Lindesmith v. Anslinger: An Early Government Victory in the Failed War on Drugs*, vol. 88 of Journal of Criminal Law and Criminology (1998), p. 681.

[3] Until this day, prohibitionists have shied away from facts and questions revealing the fallacies of their policies. This is uncontroversial, as public officials have never tolerated an open examination of the facts, and every study they have funded has been designed to bolster prohibition propaganda. Reform activists are keen to point this out. The Global Drug Policy Commission, for example, has noted that "in spite of the increasing evidence that current policies are not achieving their objectives, most policymaking bodies at the national and international level have tended to avoid open scrutiny or debate on alternatives." Former U.S. Senator Joseph L. Galiber was even blunter when, in a bill to repeal the drug laws, he stated that "criminalization of . . . drugs has fostered—indeed, even required—not enlightenment, but enforced public ignorance of the true nature of the perils of drug use. One of the more conspicuous accoutrements of our futile coercive tactics is what has been euphemistically labeled drug "education." There is nothing remotely educational about the hyperbole publicly expounded about drugs, which is little other than a medieval attempt to suppress, not reveal, knowledge. It is no more educational than Victorian efforts were to educate young males about masturbation. The metaphors have merely changed from impotence, blindness, and hairy palms to fried brains. The design is the same: terror and fright replace information. Our drug educators act as shrill propagandists instead of cultivators of inquisitive minds." Joseph L. Galiber, *A Bill to Repeal the Drug Laws: Replacing Prohibition With Regulation*, p. 14.

Professor of law Randy Barnett noted the lack of concern for prohibitionist policies: "In war, it is said, truth is the first casualty. To be blunt, many committed prohibitionists inside and outside of government who profess to care so much about the morals of others routinely lie or willfully mislead the public about nearly every aspect of both drugs and the policy of prohibition. Our consistent experience with drug prohibition—from marijuana, to heroin, to cocaine—is that when careful empirical studies are eventually performed, they reveal the initial official accounts to be either false or wildly exaggerated. Rarely, if ever, does law enforcement then reverse itself or even moderate its rhetoric." Randy Barnett, *Bad Trip: Drug Prohibition and the Weakness of Public Policy*, p. 2603. See also *supra* note 1 and *infra* notes 14, 64, 66, 70.

[4] Charles Whitebread, a professor of law who has written extensively on the subject, speaks to it thus: "The lesson is clear. Moral regulation perpetuates fear, not morality.  . . . At the core of the effort to regulate morality lies the desire of "us" to regulate "them."  With each prohibition, a socially dominant group burdens a weaker class of citizens with its notion of propriety. And notwithstanding the moral justifications used to support them, moral regulations only succeed in exacerbating existing social rifts. . . . As we enter a new century, it is abundantly clear that it is time to free ourselves from the idea of prohibition. . . . We should understand, like never before, that the idea is inherently flawed." Charles H. Whitebread, *Us and Them and the Nature of Moral Regulation*, Southern California Law Review Vol. 74:361, pp. 362-63,70. See also *infra* notes 67, 72, 73, 77, 78, 79, 80, 81, 82, 83, 84, 85, 86, 87, 88, 89, 90.

[5] The quote is taken from a report they prepared together with other members of the Global Commission on Drug Policy. For more, see the Global Commission on Drug Policy's *June 2011 report*, p. 5, 17.

[6] Douglas and McDonald, *The Prohibition of Illicit Drugs is Killing and Criminalising our Children and We are All Letting it Happen*, Report of a high level Australia 21 Roundtable (2012), p. 22.

[7] Barret et al., *Recalibrating the Regime: The Need for a Human Rights-Based Approach to International Drug Policy*, Beckley Foundation (2008), pp. 1-2.

[8] It is estimated that 10 million people around the world are imprisoned for drug-related offenses (See Bryan Stevenson, *Drug Policy, Criminal Justice,*

*and Mass Imprisonment*, Global Commission on Drug Policy working paper, prepared for January 24-25 meeting (2011). As pertains to the drug-war deaths, it is estimated that in Latin America alone, some 150,000 people are murdered every year because of prohibition (*The Drug Problem in the Americas*, Organization of American States, 2013, p. 76). Add to this numbers from the rest of the world, as well as the fact that of the estimated 160,000 drug-related deaths, some 80 percent is assumed to be systemic (i.e., a consequence of prohibition), and this number is not an exaggeration. For more, see *infra* note 80.

[9] THOMAS SZASZ, *OUR RIGHT TO DRUGS* (Praeger 1992) p. 14.

[10] David Bergland, *Libertarianism, Natural Rights and the Constitution: A Commentary on Recent Libertarian Literature*, p. 510 (available at http://engaged scholarship.csuohio.edu/clevstlrev/vol44/iss4/6).

[11] See *infra* notes 70, 71.

[12] See *infra* notes 67, 72, 73, 77, 78, 79, 80, 82, 83, 84.

[13] See *infra* note 71.

[14] In discussing the American Medical Association's role in perpetuating falsities, Professor of Psychiatry Thomas Szasz writes: "The American Medical Association's position on self-medication and drug control has at least been consistent during the past fifty years. It has never told the truth about drugs (as that 'truth' was seen and recorded by contemporary chemists and pharmacologists), if telling it was in conflict with government policies." THOMAS SZASZ, *CEREMONIAL CHEMISTRY*, p. 128. See also *supra* notes 1, 3 and *infra* notes 65, 70, 74.

[15] DAVID NUTT, *DRUGS: WITHOUT THE HOT AIR* (2012), p. 43.

[16] *Ibid*, p. 7.

[17] *Ibid*, p. 280. See also *infra* note 70.

[18] GARY NULL, C. DEAN, ET AL., *DEATH BY MEDICINE* (2003).

[19] DOUGLAS HUSAK, *LEGALIZE THIS! THE CASE FOR DECRIMINALIZING DRUGS* (2002), p. 137.

[20] ROAR MIKALSEN, *HUMAN RISING (2010)*, p. 111.

[21] For more on this, see *infra* note 78, 79, 80, 82,

[22] General Comment no. 18, paragraph 7.

[23] General Comment no. 18, paragraph 12.

[24] *Human Rights: Civil and Political Rights*, Human Rights Committee's Fact Sheet No. 15 (Rev.1) p. 7.

[25] Kent Roach, *The Primacy of Liberty and Proportionality, Not Human Dignity, When Subjecting Criminal Law to Constitutional Control*, Israeli Law Review 44:91 (2011), p.112-13.

[26] General Comment no. 18, paragraph 10.

[27] General Comment no. 18, paragraph 6.

[28] HUSAK, *LEGALIZE THIS! THE CASE FOR DECRIMINALIZING DRUGS* (2002), p. 163. See also *infra* notes 83-90.

[29] Woodrow Wilson: *Address, New York Press Club, May 9, 1912.*

[30] Hugh Brogan, *Longman History of the United States of America* (1987), p. 518.

[31] NUTT, *DRUGS: WITHOUT THE HOT AIR* (2012), p. 269. See also *infra* notes 45, 77, 78, 81.

[32] *Ibid*, p. 271. See also *infra* notes 45, 77, 78, 81.

[33] See *infra* note 80.

[34] Thomas Szasz speaks to it: "Doctors, lawyers and politicians started the War on Drugs and continue to wage it, and . . . they are its real beneficiaries. In contrast, the drug war's ostensible beneficiaries—the poor, the uneducated, the young, the old, and the sick—are its actual victims." SZASZ, *OUR RIGHT TO DRUGS* (1992), p. 157. See also *infra* note 84.

[35] Steven Wisotsky, professor of law at Nova Southeastern University, has written an article called *A Society of Suspects: The War on Drugs and our Civil Liberties* (Cato Institute Policy Analysis No. 180, 1992). He states:

"This country's Founders would be disappointed with what we have done to their legacy of liberty: The War on Drugs, by its very nature, is a war on the Bill of Rights. When the Founders rebelled against British tyranny, they grounded their cause in a belief in the natural rights of the individual and the Enlightenment ideas of progress through reason. Understanding the dangers of an excessive concentration of political power, they divided and limited the reach of that power through a federal structure with the states, the separation of powers among the three branches, and the guarantees of personal freedom in the Constitution itself and in the Bill of Rights. With the War on Drugs, however, the wisdom of the Founders has been cast aside. In their shortsighted zeal to create a 'Drug-Free America' by 1995, our political leaders—state and federal, elected and appointed—have acted as though the end justifies the means, repudiating our heritage of limited government and individual freedoms while endowing the bureaucratic state with unprecedented powers." (p. 1, sources omitted).

[36] See *infra* notes 42, 79, 80, 82.

[37] Count the Costs, *The War on Drugs: Undermining International Development and Security, Increasing Conflict*, p. 7

[38] See *infra* notes 80, 81, 82.

[39] SZASZ, *OUR RIGHT TO DRUGS* (1992), p. 136.

[40] The American Navy recognized this in a report to Congress some 50 years ago when they said: "Realistically, all wars have been for economic reasons. [But] to make the politically palatable, ideological issues have always been involved. Any possible future war will undoubtedly conform to historical precedent." GERALD COLBY, *DU PONT DYNASTY: BEHIND THE NYLON CURTAIN* (1984), p. 408.

[41] MIKALSEN, *HUMAN RISING* (2021), and NUTT: *DRUGS WITHOUT THE HOT AIR* (2012), p. 45-46 and 271-73. See also *infra* notes 64, 66, 70.

[42] "Has the War on Drugs minimised harm? The short answer is no. In fact it has done the opposite: it has increased harm for pretty much everyone. This is well known amongst policy-makers, though rarely openly acknowledged." NUTT, *DRUGS: WITHOUT THE HOT AIR* (2012), p. 273.

[43] MIKALSEN, *HUMAN RISING* (2010), p. 46.

[44] *Ibid*, p. 45.

[45] A group of experts concluded thus after looking into the subject matter: "Fairly consistently, the finding has been that changes in penalties for use have little effect on rates of use, or on problems arising from effects of the drug. In general, the attempt at deterrence of use or possession though criminal laws have failed." (Room et al. *Cannabis Policy: Moving Beyond Stalemate* (2010), p. 148). This has also been confirmed by a British Government study. In November 2014, the Home Office released its *Drugs, International Comparators* study, which looked at different approaches to drugs policy and treatment in a number of countries including some from countries that have harsh criminal sanctions for users and some that have effectively decriminalised the possession of drugs. The report found that tough criminal sentences for drug users makes no difference to the rates of drug use, being that use of illegal substances is influenced by factors "more complex and nuanced than legislation and enforcement alone" and "there is no apparent correlation between the 'toughness' of a country's approach and the prevalence of drug use." Other reports and studies confirming this are Jean-Paul Grund & Joost Breeksema, *Coffee Shops and Compromise: Separated Illicit Drug Markets in the Netherlands*, Open Society Foundations (2013); Transform, *Drug Decriminalisation in Portugal: Setting the Record Straight*, 2014; Katherine Beckett and Steve Herbert, *The Consequences and Costs of Marijuana Prohibition*, (2006); Patricia G Ericson & Benedict Fisher: *Canadian Cannabis Policy: Impact of Criminalization, the Current Reality and Future Policy Options* p. 227-242 in Lorentz Bollinger (ed.), *Cannabis Science: From Prohibition to Human Right* (1997); Artur Domosławski, *Drug Policy in Portugal: The Benefits of Decriminalizing Drug Use*, Open Society Foundations (2011); Craig Reinarman, Peter D. A. Cohen & Hendrien L. Kaal, *The Limited Relevance of Drug Policy: Cannabis in Amsterdam and in San Francisco* (2004) 94 Am. J. Pub. Health 836. For even more on this see *infra* notes 77, 78, 84.

[46] NUTT, *DRUGS WITHOUT THE HOT AIR* (2012), p. 24.

[47] HUSAK, *LEGALIZE THIS! THE CASE FOR DECRIMINALIZING DRUGS* (2002). See also *infra* notes 82-90.

[48] NUTT, *DRUGS WITHOUT THE HOT AIR* (2012), p. 23.

[49] Lysander Spooner, *Vices Are Not Crimes*, p. 1

[50] Lysander Spooner, *Vices Are Not Crimes*, p. 5.

[51] JAMES P GRAY, *WHY OUR DRUG LAWS HAVE FAILED AND WHAT WE CAN DO ABOUT IT* (2001), p. 122.

[52] RONALD IRVING, *THE LAW IS AN ASS* (2010), p. 269.

[53] B.C. Nirmal, *Natural Law, Human Rights and Justice: Some Reflections on Finnis's Natural Law Theory*, p 26.

[54] UNDP, UNAIDS, WHO, *International Guidelines on Human Rights and Drug Policy* (2020) p. 7

[55] MADS ANDENÆS, ERIK BJØRGE, *MENNESKERETTENE OG OSS* (2012), p. 33

[56] General Comment no. 35, paragraph 12.

[57] Drug analyst James Ostrowski estimates that 80% of the world's 160,000 drug-use-deaths are caused by prohibition, while only 20% by the inherent qualities of the drugs (Ostrowski, *The Moral and Practical Case for Drug Legalization*, p. 654). For more on the destructive effects of prohibition, see *infra* notes 79, 80.

[58] See GRINSPOON & BAKALAR, *PSYCHEDELIC DRUGS RECONSIDERED*; ROAR MIKALSEN, *REASON IS*; ROBERT FORTE, *ENTHEOGENS AND THE FUTURE OF RELIGION*; CHRISTOPHER GRAY, *THE ACID DIARIES*; STANISLAV GROF, *REALMS OF THE HUMAN UNCONSCIOUS*; STANISLAV GROF, *LSD: DOORWAY TO THE NUMINOUS*; STANISLAV GROF, *THE COSMIC GAME: EXPLORATIONS OF THE FRONTIERS OF HUMAN CONSCIOUSNESS*; NEAL GOLDSMITH, *PSYCHEDELIC HEALING*; RICK STRASSMAN, *DMT: THE SPIRIT MOLECULE*.

[59] ROBERT FORTE, *ENTHEOGENS AND THE FUTURE OF RELIGION* (Park Street Press) 2012, p. 4.

[60] *Ibid*, p. 186.

[61] Allison Brandi Margolin, *On the Right to Get High* (2002) p. 37.

[62] FORTE, *ENTHEOGENS AND THE FUTURE OF RELIGION* (Park Street Press, 2012), p. 189. See also MIKALSEN, *REASON IS*.

[63] General Comment 11, paragraph 2.

[64] GRAY, *WHY OUR DRUG LAWS HAVE FAILED AND WHAT WE CAN DO ABOUT IT: A JUDICIAL INDICTMENT OF THE WAR ON DRUGS* (Temple University Press 2001), p. 11.

[65] Examples of responsible marijuana studies available in the 1930s include the Indian Hemp Drugs Commission of 1893-94, and Siler et al., *Marijuana Smoking in Panama*. The findings of such commissions were either ignored or attacked by enforcement officials committed to the contrary position. For more on this, see Lester Grinspoon, *Marihuana Reconsidered* (Harvard University Press) 1977, pp. 27-29. See also *supra* notes 1, 3, 14, and *infra* notes 65, 66, 70, 74.

[66] In the Journal of Criminal Law and Criminology vol. 88 (1998) John F. Galliher, David P. Keys, and Michael Elsner documents in *Lindesmith v. Anslinger: An Early Government Victory in the Failed War on Drugs* how prohibitionists intimidated and fought those who opposed their deceitful propaganda. See also *supra* notes 1, 3, 14, 64 and *infra* notes 66, 70, 74.

[67] See WILLIAM J. STUNTZ, *THE COLLAPSE OF AMERICAN CRIMINAL JUSTICE* (Harvard University Press, 2011); WILLIAM J. CHAMBLISS & ROBERT B. SEIDMAN, *LAW, ORDER, AND POWER* (1971); and ROBERT P. RHODES, *THE INSOLUBLE PROBLEMS OF CRIME* (1977). In *Rationalizing Drug Policy under Federalism* (pp. 711-21) professors David W. Rasmussen & Bruce L. Benson analyze current policy as a result of bureaucratic self-interest. They conclude: "In a representative democracy there is a tendency to expect that public opinion drives drug policy. This is not the case, as every detailed study of the emergence of legal norms has consistently shown the immense importance of interest-group activity, not the public interest, as the critical variable. Drug war, the excessive application of enforcement that aggravates rather than mitigates the social consequences of drug use, is waged because it is in the interests of particular politically influential groups, including law

enforcement bureaucracies and public officials. According to this view, legislators can act as moral entrepreneurs, but they are more generally "middle-men" whose actions are largely determined by interest groups, including those engaged in the law enforcement process—police chiefs, sheriffs, and prosecutors."(p. 711)

The same conclusion, that the war on drugs persists because of bureaucratic self-interest, is found in Bruce L. Benson, *The War on Drugs: A Public Bad* (2008), pp. 36-50. For more on how prohibitionists, until today, have ignored scientific advice and concealed the facts in order to maintain their flawed policies, see Judge Robert Sweet's lecture in *Towards a Compassionate and Cost-effective Drug Policy: A Forum on the Impact of Drug Policy on the Justice System and Human Rights*, Fordham Urban Law Journal Vol. 24, Issue 2 (1996), pp. 319-30; Laurent Laniel, *The Relationship between Research and Drug Policy in the United States*, Management of Social Transformations, Discussion Paper No. 44; Blumenson & Nilsen, *No Rational Basis: The Pragmatic Case for Marijuana Law Reform* (2009), pp. 12-16; and Rolles (ed.), *A Comparison of the Cost-effectiveness of Prohibition and Regulation of Drugs*, Transform Drug Policy Foundation (April 2009), pp.14-15. See also *supra* notes 1, 3, 14, 64, 65 and *infra* notes 70, 74.

[68] For literature calling for the decriminalization of drugs/victimless crimes from a perspective of efficiency-based arguments, see JOHN KAPLAN, *MARIJUANA: THE NEW PROHIBITION* (1970); NORVAL MORRIS & GORDON HAWKINS, *THE HONEST POLITICIAN'S GUIDE TO CRIME CONTROL* (1970); HERBERT PACKER, *THE LIMITS OF THE CRIMINAL SANCTION* (1968); Kadish, *The Crisis of Overcriminalization*; Steven B. Duke, *The Future of Marijuana in the United States* (2013); Steven B. Duke, *Drug Prohibition: An Unnatural Disaster*; Daniel D. Polsby, *Ending the War on Drugs and Children*; John J. Donohue et al., *Rethinking America's Illegal Drug Policy* in Philip J. Cook, Jens Ludwig, and Justin McCrary (ed.), *Controlling Crime: Strategies and Tradeoffs*; Blumenson & Nilsen, *No Rational Basis: The Pragmatic Case for Marijuana Law Reform* (2009); Rasmussen & Benson, *Rationalizing Drug Policy under Federalism*. For a cost-benefit analysis of prohibition versus legalization, see Rolles (ed.), *A Comparison of*

*the Cost-effectiveness of Prohibition and Regulation of Drugs*, Transform Drug Policy Foundation (April 2009).

This approach, however, fails to give adequate weight to the dignity of persons, and for a more comprehensive defense of legalization on both moral and cost-benefit grounds, see James Ostrowski, *The Moral and Practical Case for Drug Legalization*, Hofstra Law Review, Vol. 18:607 (1990). See also *infra* notes 78, 80.

[69] See for example Samuel Freeman's article *Liberalism, Inalienability, and Rights of Drug Use*, in PABLO DE GREIFF (ED.), *DRUGS AND THE LIMITS OF LIBERALISM: MORAL AND LEGAL ISSUES* (1999); DOUGLAS HUSAK, *DRUGS AND RIGHTS*; DOUGLAS HUSAK, *LEGALIZE THIS: THE CASE FOR DECRIMINALIZING DRUGS*; Roger Pilon, *The Illegitimate War on Drugs*, in Timothy Lynch (ed.), *After Prohibition: an Adult Approach to Drug Policies in the 21st Century* (2000); Andrew Koppelman, *Drug Policy and the Liberal Self*; DAVID A.J. RICHARDS, *SEX, DRUGS, DEATH, AND THE LAW*; David Bergland, *Libertarianism, Natural Rights and the Constitution: A Commentary on Recent Libertarian Literature*; Warren Redlich, *A Substantive Due Process Challenge to the War on Drugs*; Eva Nilsen & Eric Blumenson, *Liberty Lost: the Moral Case for Marijuana Law Reform*; THOMAS SZASZ, *OUR RIGHT TO DRUGS*; Walter Block, *Drug Prohibition: A Legal and Economic Analysis* (1993).

[70] MIKALSEN, *REASON IS* (2014).

[71] For more on the harmfulness of licit and illicit drugs, see for instance DUKE AND GROSS, *AMERICA'S LONGEST WAR*. This epic work compares the harmfulness of tobacco and alcohol with marijuana, heroin, and cocaine. The authors compare each drug's physical and psychological effects, its criminogenic effects, and its positive and negative health consequences. The legal ones are shown to be worse than the illegal ones. When it comes to marijuana, not only alcohol and tobacco but obesity is far more damaging to the human body, and on pages 74-77 statistics are presented suggesting that per 100,000 users, the following numbers are killed by their drug of choice every year: tobacco 650; alcohol 150; heroin 80; cocaine 4; marijuana 0.

Similar comparisons revealing the irrational separation between licit and illicit drugs are found in the Global Cannabis Commission Report, *Cannabis Policy: Moving Beyond Stalemate*, Beckley Foundation (2008), pp. 52-55; James Ostrowski, *The Moral and Practical Case for Drug Legalization*, Hofstra Law Review: Vol. 18:607 (1990), pp. 688-702; and the Journal of the American Medical Association 270 (18) (1993), pp. 2207–12. In the latter, Michael McGinnis and William Foege's article *Actual Causes of Death in the United States*, concludes that Americans are twenty-five times more likely to die from the use of tobacco and alcohol than they are from the use of illicit drugs.

Another scientific study investigated the severity of addiction and withdrawal across six psychoactive drugs (caffeine, nicotine, alcohol, heroin, cocaine, and marijuana). This study concluded that marijuana and caffeine were the least addictive of these substances, asserting that marijuana is "slightly less addictive than caffeine. (See Zimmer L.E., and Morgan J.P., *Marijuana myths, marijuana facts: a review of the scientific evidence*, Bookworld Services, 1997.)

A World Health Organization study adds to this picture. In 2000, it estimated a range of major risk factors and concluded that the proportion of the total burden of disease in the Western European region attributable to tobacco was 12.2%, alcohol 9.2%, and illicit drugs 1,8%. (Robin Room, *The Public Health Significance of Cannabis in the Spectrum of Psychoactive substances* in EMCDDA, *A Cannabis Reader: Global Issues and Local Experiences*, Monograph series 8, Vol. 2, 2008, p. 147.) On a global scale, the WHO estimated in 2001 that illicit drug use accounted for approximately 0,6% of all lost disability-adjusted life years (DALYs) (all causes), compared to 6.1% caused by alcohol and tobacco. (WHO, *The Global Burden of Disease*; Alan D. Lopez, Epidemiologyand Burden of Disease Team, World Health Organization. 2020 Focus 5, Brief 2, February 2001.)

Other articles comparing the harms of licit and illicit drugs include Nutt et al., *Development of a Rational Scale to Assess the Harm of Drugs of Potential Misuse*, Lancet 369 (2007), pp. 1047–53; Gable, *Comparison of Acute Lethal Toxicity of Commonly Abused Psychoactive Substances*, Addiction 99 (2004), pp. 686–96; the Lancet editorial *Dangerous Habits*, the Lancet no. 9140 (1998); van Amsterdam, Opperhuizen, Koeter & van den

Brink, *Ranking the Harm of Alcohol, Tobacco and Illicit Drugs for the Individual and the Population*, Eur Addict Res 16 (2010),  pp. 202–27; as well as the discussion paper *A Public Health Approach to Drug Control in Canada*, Health Officers Council of British Columbia (October 2005) pp. 6-8. The latter mentions interesting findings: "Single et al compared the deaths and diseases caused by alcohol, tobacco and illegal drug use in Canada. They found that alcohol, tobacco, and illegal drugs accounted for 20.0% of all deaths, 22.2% of years of all potential life lost, and 9.4% of all admissions to hospital in Canada in 1995. Of all substances, tobacco was by far the largest contributor to mortality, making up 83% of deaths, while alcohol accounted for 16% and illegal drugs only 2% respectively. The PYLL (potential years of life lost) proportions reflect the younger age profile of deaths due to illegal drugs and to alcohol-related injuries, with alcohol making up 24% of PYLL, illegal drugs 5% and tobacco 71%. By any measure tobacco is the dominant contributor to health related harms."(p. 6-7, sources omitted)

The report by Single et al. estimated the costs of substance abuse in Canada. Alcohol accounted for more than $7.5 billion in costs, representing 40.8% of the total costs of substance abuse, and tobacco accounted for $9.56 billion in costs. This was more than half (51.8%) of the total substance abuse costs, while the economic costs of illegal drugs were estimated at $1.37 billion (7.4%). It must be noted that much of these costs must be attributed to prohibition. The costs of enforcement, for instance, totaled some $400 million; much of the cost attributed to lost productivity was because of people serving jail time; and much of the disease and premature death was due to prohibition-related effects. The discussion paper goes on to note: "The larger societal economic costs due to alcohol and tobacco have been replicated in recent reviews in other countries. Collins and Lapsley found costs in Australia of $34.7 Billion (AU) per annum, that were proportionally 61% due to tobacco, 22% due to alcohol, and 17% due to illegal drugs. In France in 1997, proportional costs of 41%, 53% and 6% respectively were found due to tobacco, alcohol and illegal drugs, out of a total societal cost of 218 Billion franc per year. Harwood found in the United States the costs in 1992 were US$148 Billion related to alcohol, and US$98 Billion related to illegal drugs. These studies were consistent in that the greater economic losses for alcohol and tobacco were due to lost productivity, whereas for illegal drugs the costs related more to enforcement."(pp. 7-8, sources omitted)

Another article which summarizes a great deal of the research (as of 2008) is Robin Room, *The Public Health Significance of Cannabis in the Spectrum of Psychoactive substances* (see EMCDDA, *A Cannabis Reader: Global Issues and Local Experiences*, Monograph series 8, Vol. 2, 2008, pp. 146-54.). This paper not only shows how the licit drugs are worse than many illicit drugs, but how prohibitionists have tried to obscure the facts. As he says: "There is an enormous commitment by many involved in the international control system and equivalent national systems to keeping the status quo, [and so] comparing degrees of dangerousness is a fraught topic. General comparisons of this type have often faced substantial opposition in the course of publication. [For instance], the material from the Prime Minister's Strategy Unit was only released on 1 July 2005, 2 years after compilation, in partial compliance with a Freedom of Information request. The report by Hall et al. was eventually published after a media storm over its omission from the [WHO] report for which it was originally commissioned. The Roques report also caused considerable controversy when it appeared. As a French review noted, there were complaints not only about including alcohol among 'drugs', but also that the group of experts 'banalized the danger of cannabis by putting in evidence the weak physical and psychic dependence from this product, compared with those of tobacco and alcohol'." EMCDDA, *A Cannabis Reader: Global Issues and Local Experiences*, Monograph series 8, Vol. 2, 2008, p. 153,152, (Sources omitted).

Still, despite attempts to sabotage evidence-based policies, more and more research is publicized. The most comprehensive study was performed by the Independent Scientific Committee on Drugs in 2010 (see Nutt et al., *Drug harms in the UK: a Multicriteria Decision Analysis*, Lancet 2010; 376: pp. 1558–65). This study is discussed in NUTT, *DRUGS: WITHOUT THE HOT AIR*, where Nutt is careful to note that the social, health, and economic costs associated with licit drugs are far greater than the illicit ones. A 2015 study by Dirk W. Lachenmeier and Jürgen Rehm performed a comparative risk assessment study of licit and illicit drugs using the margin of exposure

(MOE) approach and the main finding was the qualitative validation of previous expert-based approaches on drug-ranking (like ISCD's 2010 study above), especially in regard to the positions of alcohol (highest) and cannabis (lowest).

In addition to this, the irrationality of the classification system has been pointed out by many other experts, including Margaret P. Battin, Erik Luna, Arthur G. Lipman, Paul M. Gahlinger, Douglas E. Rollins, Jeanette C. Roberts, and Troy L. Booher. In their book *DRUGS AND JUSTICE: SEEKING A CONSISTENT, COHERENT, COMPREHENSIVE VIEW*, (Oxford University Press 2008), the authors argue that the entire classification system must be revised if policy is to be evidence-based. As they state: "The argument that differences in regulatory rationales are designed to track differences in drugs is not supported by pharmacology or actual practice. Such an argument might be plausible if differing types of drugs were classified consistently according to an intelligible, well-reasoned, consistent, and coherent schema. Yet much of the current drug classification and thus assignment to a particular agency appears to be the product of politically motivated historical events, rather than by the properties of the drugs themselves or their effects in users." (p. 88)

". . . Some illegal drugs present little risk of harm to the user or to others but are nonetheless listed in the Controlled Substances Act. Many, if not most, of these drugs are hallucinogens. LSD, peyote, DMT, psilocybin, mescaline, and marijuana do not present major biological risks of harm to the user, are not physically addictive, and present no evident harm to others when taken in an appropriate setting." (p.172)

"It would be tempting to say that these misclassifications are at the root of any conceptual and practical trouble over drugs. Indeed, these misclassifications do play a major role, and they are the focal point for much of the contemporary critique of drug policy. Recognizing these misclassifications, based on inappropriate and inadequate rationales for the categorization of specific drugs, presents a major opportunity for reclassification and thus the development of more consistent, coherent, comprehensive drug theory and policy." (p. 159)

"We must make significant changes, not merely cosmetic prunings, in the way we treat drugs—all drugs. This means scrapping many of the laws now on the books and starting over."(p. 258)

Also reports like *A Fresh Approach to Drugs*, UK Drug Policy Commission (October 2012) and the *Report of the Global Commission on Drug Policy* (June 2011) recommend a total revision of the classification system. See also House of Commons Science and Technology Committee, Drug classification: Making a Hash of It? Fifth Report of Session (2005–06), pp. 3-50, for more on its lack of merit.

[72] Research indicates that the vast majority of people who use illegal drugs, (like the vast majority of people who use legal drugs) do so without creating problems. The United Nations, for instance, estimates that there are 250 million drug users worldwide, of which less than 10 percent is considered to be problem drug users. (Report of the Global Commission on Drug Policy (June, 2011), p.13)

The illicit drugs' addictive and destructive properties, therefore, are vastly misrepresented, which Arnold S. Trebach's, *The Heroin Solution* (Yale University Press, 1982) says more about. In this book statistics are presented which indicate that, while the U.S. had 500,000 heroin addicts in the late 1970's, there were 3,500,000 non-addicted occasional users. This suggests a 12.5% addiction rate, which is confirmed by looking at the numbers in Great Britain. While 0.9 percent of people aged 16-59 had tried opiates, only 0.1 percent reported having used them in the last year. (Peter Reuter & Alex Stevens, *An Analysis of UK Drug Policy: A Monograph Prepared for the UK Drug Policy Commission*, 2007, pp. 20-21)

Last year use, of course, does not necessarily mean that they are problem users, as quite a few can control their use of heroin, contradicting popular notions that addiction is an inevitable consequence of heroin use. Several studies confirm this. For more information see Warburton et al., *Occasional and controlled heroin use: Not a problem?* York: Joseph Rowntree Foundation (2005) and D. Shewan & P. Dalgarno, *Evidence for controlled heroin use? Low levels of negative health and social outcomes among non-treatment heroin users in Glasgow (Scotland)*, British Journal of Health Psychology, 10, (2006), pp. 33–48.

Some laboratory studies show a higher rate, but these studies use medical grade, pure heroin. In *Health Consequences of Smoking: Nicotine Addiction* (Surgeon General's Report, 1988), a comparison is made of the relative addictiveness of smoked tobacco and several other drugs. According to this report alcohol has a 15% addiction rate, while tobacco is credited with an addiction rate of 90%. The Surgeon General's Report also observes that of the US soldiers who became addicted to heroin in Vietnam, approximately 90% were able to avoid readdiction upon return to the U.S. Another source of statistics is an article entitled *Hooked, not Hooked* by Deborah Franklin (In Health magazine Nov/Dec 1990). This article cites addiction experts' rankings of various legal and illegal drugs as follows: (1) Nicotine, (2) Crack, (3) Valium, (4) Alcohol, (5) Heroin, (6) Cocaine, (7) Caffeine, (8) Marijuana, (9) Ecstasy, (10) Psilocybin Mushrooms and LSD.

In Eric Goode, *Drugs in American Society* (1999) pp. 129-30, of people who have taken an alcoholic drink at least once in their lives, 62% have done so in the past month; the figures for cigarettes are 40%; marijuana 15%; heroin 9%; cocaine 8%; stimulants 9%; and hallucinogens 7%. In Philip J. Cook, Jens Ludwig, and Justin McCrary (ed.), *Controlling Crime: Strategies and Tradeoffs,* John J. Donohue et al. compare alcohol and cannabis (see *Rethinking America's Illegal Drug Policy* pp. 244-269) citing reports that deal with addiction rates, harms, and patterns of use. Among other studies, they cite research in a N.Y. Times article by Kershaw and Cathcart, suggesting that 10 percent of cannabis users, 15 percent of alcohol users, 15 percent of cocaine users, 25 percent of heroin users, and 33 percent of tobacco smokers will develop addiction.

Speaking of addiction and drugs' ability to destroy lives, we must keep in mind that *how* the drug is experienced depends on psychological, *not* pharmacological properties. For more on this, see Richard G. Schlaadt and Peter T. Shannon, *Drugs: Use, Misuse, and Abuse.* We should also keep in mind that there is no real distinction between drug and nondrug addictions (see for instance Lance Dodes, *The Heart of Addiction*) and that studies in the addictionology literature have found that 9 percent of the entire population will be addicted to something (not only drugs) at some point in their lives. For more on this, see David A. Fishbain, *Chronic Opioid*

*Treatment: Addiction and Pseudo-Addiction in Patients with Chronic Pain*, Psychiatric Times (2003) at http://www.psychiatrictimes.com/p030225.html.

For more on addiction, see JAMES B. BAKALAR & LESTER GRINSPOON, *DRUG CONTROL IN A FREE SOCIETY*, Cambridge University Press (1998), p. 35-67, and for more on patterns of use, see Thomas Nicholson et al., *Is Recreational Drug Use Normal?*; Ethan A. Nadelmann, *Drug Prohibition in the United States: Costs, Consequences, and Alternatives*; M.E. Jarvik, *The Drug Dilemma: Manipulating the Demand*; A. Goldstein, & H. Kalant, *Drug Policy: Striking the Right Balance*; C. Winick, *Social Behavior, Public Policy, and Nonharmful Drug Use*; Steven B. Duke, *Drug Prohibition: An Unnatural Disaster* pp. 29-37.

[73] The list of professionals is too long to describe. After all, it includes just about everyone who knows a thing or two about drug policy. However, to give an idea, a group of 500 luminaries from around the world—including Nobel Laureate Milton Friedman, former Secretary of State George Shultz, and former UN Secretary General Javier Perez de Cueller—have signed an open letter the U.S. President and Congress arguing that the global war on drugs is causing more harm than good and urging that alternatives be considered. Another group of 770 academics wrote to the UN Secretary General in 1998, declaring that "the global war on drugs is now causing more harm than drug abuse itself", and asking the bureaucrats "to initiate a truly open and honest dialogue regarding the future of global drug control policies; one in which fear, prejudice and punitive prohibitions yield to common sense, science, public health and human rights". (see http://www.drugpolicy.org/publications-resources/sign-letters/public-letter-kofi-annan/ungass-public-letter-kofi-annan-signato)

For other signatory campaigns, see the work of the Global Commission of Drug Policy, a group of statesmen and academics who say exactly the same. Other examples include Isaac Campos, a drug historian at the University of Cincinnati; Jeffrey Miron, an economist at Harvard University; economists David W. Rasmussen and Bruce L. Benson; Jefferson M. Fish, a professor emeritus of psychology; Thomas Szasz, another distinguished psychiatrist; Scholars of law such as John J. Donohue III, Steven B. Duke, Albert C. Gross, Harry G. Levine, Douglas Husak,

Richard Glen Boire, Marc J. Blitz, Roger Pilon, Michelle Alexander, Randy E. Barnett, James Ostrowski, Andrew Koppelman, David A.J. Richards, Doug Bandow, David Bergland, Paul Hager, Allison Brandi Margolin, Michèle Alexandre, Warren Redlich, Merle Anouk de Vries, Erik Luna, Eva Nilsen and Eric Blumenson have all written on the subject; Herbert Packer, a Stanford Law School professor, argued likewise already in the 1960's; so did Charles H. Whitebread, a professor of law at the University of Southern California, and Steven Wisotsky also said so in a prepared statement before the Select Committee on Narcotics Abuse and Control, House of Representatives, September 29th, 1988. The list goes on.

[74] *Marijuana: A Signal of Misunderstanding*, National Commission on Marihuana and Drug Abuse (1972); *Legislative Options for Cannabis in Australia: Report on the National Task Force on Cannabis*, Australian National Drug Strategy Committee (1994); *A Wiser Course: Ending Drug Prohibition*, New York City Bar Association (1994); *Drug Lore: The Questioning of our Current Drug Law*, Australian Drug Law Reform Foundation (1996); *Cannabis: Our Position for a Public Policy*, Canadian Senate Special Committee on Illegal Drugs (Sept. 4, 2002); Rolles et al., *After the War on Drugs: Options for Control*, Transform Drug Policy Foundation (2004); *A Public Health Approach to Drug Control in Canada*, Health Officers Council of British Columbia (October 2005); Katherine Beckett and Steve Herbert, *The Consequences and Costs of Marijuana Prohibition*, (2006); *The Failure of the War on Drugs: Charting a New Course for the Commonwealth*, Report of the Massachusetts Bar Association Drug Task Force (2008); *After the War on Drugs: Blueprint for Regulation*, Transform Drug Policy Foundation (2009); Werb et al., *Effect of Drug Law Enforcement on Drug-Related Violence: Evidence from a Scientific Review*, International Centre for Science in Drug Policy (2010); *The War on Drugs Has Failed: It is Time for a New Approach*, Global Commission on Drug Policy (17 November 2011); Peter Hakim, *Rethinking US Drug Policy*, Inter-American Dialogue/the Beckley Foundation (2011); Oscapella et al., *Changing the Frame: A New Approach to Drug Policy in Canada*, Canadian Drug Policy Coalition (January 2012); *A Fresh Approach to Drugs*, UK Drug Policy Commission (October 2012); *Drugs and Democracy: Toward a*

*Paradigm Shift*, Statement by the Latin American Commission on Drugs and Democracy; The Alternative World Drug Report: *Counting the Costs of the War on Drugs* (2012); *Governing the Global Drug Wars*, London School of Economics (October 2012); Bob Douglas and David McDonald, *The Prohibition of Illicit Drugs is Killing and Criminalising our Children and We are All Letting it Happen*, Report of a high level Australia 21 Roundtable Debate (2012); *An Exit Strategy for the Failed War on Drugs: A Federal Legislative Guide*, Drug Policy Alliance (2013); *Getting to Tomorrow: A Report on Canadian Drug Policy*, Canadian Drug Policy Coalition (2013); *The Drug Problem in the Americas*, Organization of American States (2013); Rep. Earl Blumenauer & Rep. Jared Polis, *The Path Forward: Rethinking Federal Marijuana Policy* (2013); Ilona Szabo de Carvalho, *Latin America Awakes: A Review of the New Drug Policy*, NOREF report (2013); *Blueprint for a Public Health and Safety Approach to Drug Policy*, DPA/NYAM (2013); *Taking Control: Pathways to Drug Policies that Work*, Global Commission on Drug Policy (2014); *Proposed Amendment of UN Drug Treaties*, LEAP (2014); Youngers & Correa (ed.), *In Search of Rights: Drug Users and State Responses in Latin America*, Colectivo de Estudios Drogas y Derecho, (2014); WACD, *Not Just in Transit: Drugs, the State and Society in West Africa*, An Independent Report of the West Africa Commission on Drugs (June 2014); Global Commission on Drug Policy, *Taking Control: Pathways to Drug Policies that Work* (2014).

[75] It has been established that the move to regulate marijuana was motivated in large part by racism and xenophobia. See, e.g., Martin D. Carcieri, *Obama, the Fourteenth Amendment, and the Drug War*, 44 Akron Law Review, 303, 325 (2011). In *Sex, Drugs, Death, and the Law*, Professor David A.J. Richards points out that "The campaign leading to the passage of the Marihuana Tax Act of 1937. . . included remarkable distortions of the evidence of harm caused by marijuana, ignoring the findings of empirical inquiries."(p.164, sources omitted). For further analysis of the irrationality surrounding marijuana prohibition in the United States, see Bonnie & Whitebread, *The Forbidden Fruit and the Tree of Knowledge: An Inquiry into the Legal History of American Marijuana Prohibition*; LESTER

GRINSPOON, *MARIHUANA RECONSIDERED* (Harvard University Press 1977), pp. 10-29; or Bonnie & Whitebread, *The Marijuana Conviction: A History of Marijuana Prohibition in the United States* (1974), where they conclude that "logic, science and philosophy have had almost nothing to do with the evolution of drug policy." (pp. 298-299). See also JACK HERER, *THE EMPEROR WEARS NO CLOTHES*; STEVEN B. DUKE & ALBERT C. GROSS, *AMERICA'S LONGEST WAR: RETHINKING OUR TRAGIC CRUSADE AGAINST DRUGS*; Matthew A. Christiansen, *A Great Schism: Social Norms and Marijuana Prohibition*, 4 Harvard Law & Policy Review. 229, 235 (2010); Roar Mikalsen, *Human Rising* (2021).

It should also be noted that cannabis entered the international drug control regime on equally dubious grounds. As quoted in *The Rise and Decline of Cannabis Prohibition: The History of Cannabis in the UN Drug Control System and Options for Reform*, Transnational Institute/Global Drug Policy Observatory (2014): "Subsequently, under the United Nations, the decision to place cannabis in Schedules I and IV of the 1961 Single Convention was heavily influenced by a memo expressing the very biased personal opinion of the WHO official Pablo Osvaldo Wolff, [a close associate of Harry Anslinger], and not based on a position taken by the WHO Expert Committee on Drug Dependence (ECDD). Although many delegates misread his paper as the WHO position, in fact the Expert Committee never presented a formal recommendation to the CND about the scheduling of cannabis; not prior to the Single Convention or, indeed, ever. . . . In itself, the absence of a WHO recommendation is sufficient reason to question the legitimacy of the current classification of cannabis on procedural grounds. A group of academic experts, including WHO researchers, recently concluded as much in *Drug and Alcohol Dependence*: "The present situation in which several important substances (e.g., cannabis, cannabis resin, heroin and cocaine) were never evaluated or were evaluated up to eight decades ago seriously undermines and delegitimizes their international control." (p. 4-5, sources omitted)

For more on this, see JACOB SULLUM, *SAYING YES: IN DEFENSE OF DRUG USE*; DAVID F. MUSTO, *THE AMERICAN DISEASE: ORIGINS OF NARCOTICS CONTROL*; James T. Bennett & Thomas J. Dilorenzo, *Official Lies: How Washington Misled Us* (1992) pp. 237-39; MIKALSEN, *HUMAN RISING*;

ROBINSON & SCHERLEN, *LIES, DAMN LIES AND DRUG WAR STATISTICS;* DORIS MARIE PROVINE, *UNEQUAL UNDER LAW: RACE IN THE WAR ON DRUGS;* and Deborah Ahrens, *Drug Panics in The Twenty-First Century; Ecstasy, Prescription Drugs, And The Reframing Of The War On Drugs.* For more on unscientific classification, prohibitionist propaganda, censure and biased agencies, see Martin Jelsma, *Drugs in the UN system: the Unwritten History of the 1998 United Nations General Assembly Special Session on Drugs,* International Journal of Drug Policy 14 (2003) p. 181-195; Matt Winterbourne, *United States Drug Policy: The scientific, Economic, and Social Issues Surrounding Marijuana* (2012); and Christopher Hallam, Dave Bewley-Taylor & Martin Jelsma, *Scheduling in the International Drug Control System,* Series on Legislative Reform of Drug Policies No. 25, TNI IDPC (June 2014). See also *supra* notes 1, 3, 14, 64, 65, 66, 70, and *infra* note 7.

[76] Professors Nilsen and Blumenson: "According to current knowledge, marijuana satisfies none of the three Schedule 1 requirements:  it (1) has a low potential for harm and abuse; (2) appears to have therapeutic benefit, as the government itself claimed in its successful patent application; and (3) according to the American College of Physicians, may be used safely under appropriate conditions." Blumenson & Nilsen, *No Rational Basis: The Pragmatic Case for Marijuana Law Reform* (2009), p. 26, sources omitted. See also the Global Cannabis Commission Report, *Cannabis Policy: Moving Beyond Stalemate,* Beckley Foundation (2008), p. 52-55; Kimani Paul-Emile, *Making Sense of Drug Regulation: A Theory of Law for Drug Control Policy,* Cornell Journal of Law & Public Policy vol. 19:691, (2010), an article that shows how drugs are regulated without relying upon scientific or medical evidence regarding the pharma-cological properties of the drugs; New York City Bar Association, *A Wiser Course: Ending Drug Prohibition, Fifteen Years Later* and *supra* notes 70, 74.

[77]   See   MIKALSEN,   *HUMAN   RISING*   (2010)   p.   393,   or http://www.encod.org/info/THE-CANNABIS-TRIBUNAL-IN-THE-HAGUE.html

[78] To quote drug researchers Peter Reuter & Alex Stevens: "Overall, the international evidence suggests that drug laws do not have direct effects on the prevalence of drug use." *(Reuter & Stevens, An Analysis of UK Drug Policy: A Monograph Prepared for the UK Drug Policy Commission*, 2007, p. 61) This is uncontroversial among drug policy experts. As a matter of fact, drugs today are cheaper, of better quality, and more available than before, while drug use is more widespread. In other words, by every measure the war on drugs has failed in its stated objectives. For more on this, see the World Drug Report of 2008; EMCDDA, *A Cannabis Reader: Global Issues and Local Experiences*, Monograph series 8, Vol. 1 and 2, European Monitoring Centre for Drugs and Drug Addiction (2008); the Report of the Global Commission on Drug Policy (June 2011) p. 4; Werb et al., *Effect of Drug Law Enforcement on Drug-Related Violence: Evidence from a Scientific Review*, International Centre for Science in Drug Policy (2010), p. 19; Eric Blumenson, *Recovering from Drugs and the Drug War: an Achievable Public Health Alternative* (2003), p. 2; Warren Redlich, *A Substantive Due Process Challenge to the War on Drugs* (p. 12-15); *supra* note 45 and *infra* note 78, 81.

[79] As the quote by Stevens and Reuter *supra* note 77 indicates, the evidence suggests that the degree of criminalization has little effect on the prevalence of drug use. Cannabis use among Dutch citizens, for instance, is lower than in many other countries, even though it has been legally available the last four decades. For more on this, see the Global Cannabis Commission Report, *Cannabis Policy: Moving Beyond Stalemate*, Beckley Foundation (2008), p. 60, showing that neighboring countries like France, Germany, and UK have higher prevalence of past year and lifetime marijuana use (this also includes USA, Canada, and Australia), as well as pp. 128-49 summarizing a series of survey findings. See also EMCDDA, *European Drug Report: Trends and Developments* (2014), p. 77; Robert MacCoun and Peter Reuter, *Assessing Drug Prohibition and Its Alternatives: A Guide for Agnostics*, Annual Review of Law and Social Science, Vol. 7 (2011), pp. 61-78; John J. Donohue et al., *Rethinking America's Illegal Drug Policy* in Philip J. Cook, Jens Ludwig, and Justin McCrary (ed.), *Controlling Crime: Strategies and Tradeoffs*, pp. 250-52. The latter also finds that Portugal, more than a

decade after decriminalizing the possession of all drugs, continues to have one of Europe's lowest prevalence of Cocaine and Cannabis use (p. 252).

In fact, research across the board suggests that the further we move away from the law-and-order approach, the better off we are. Dr Alex Wodak, president of the Australian Drug Law Reform Foundation and former president of the International Harm Reduction Association mentions one of the studies: "The best evidence that the management of heroin dependence with controlled and prescribed heroin availability made a difference, is a study published in the Lancet in 2006. This study was based on the city of Zurich. This showed that between 1992 and 2002 the number of new heroin users in Zurich was reduced from 850 in 1990 to 150 in 2002. Corresponding with that was a decrease in drug overdose deaths, a decrease in HIV infections among injecting drug users, a decrease in crime and a decrease in the quantities of heroin seized. Clearly, what was happening was that people were moving from black market heroin to white market methadone and white market heroin. This showed that treatment does work at a population level." Douglas and McDonald, *The Prohibition of Illicit Drugs is Killing and Criminalising our Children and We are All Letting it Happen*, Report of a high level Australia 21 Roundtable (2012), p. 10. For more on this and other case studies, see the June 2011 report of the Global Commission on Drug Policy, pp. 7, 10-11. See also *supra* note 45. For more on the situation in Portugal, ten years after decriminalization of all drugs, see Artur Domosławski, *Drug Policy in Portugal: The Benefits of Decriminalizing Drug Use*, Open Society Foundations (2011); and Transform Drug Policy Foundation, *Drug Decriminalisation in Portugal: Setting the Record Straight* (2014). For more on the situation in the Netherlands, 40 years after the sale of cannabis products was legalized, see Jean-Paul Grund & Joost Breeksema, *Coffee Shops and Compromise: Separated Illicit Drug Markets in the Netherlands*, Open Society Foundations (2013); Transform, *How to Regulate Cannabis: A Practical Guide* (2014); and Robert J. MacCoun, *What Can We Learn from the Dutch Cannabis Coffeeshop Experience?*, RAND (2010). For more on the situation in Switzerland, see Joanne Csete, *From the Mountaintops: What the World Can Learn from Drug Policy Change in Switzerland*, Open Society Foundations (2010); For more on the recent trends towards decriminalization worldwide, see Rosmarin & Eastwood, *A Quiet Revolution: Drug Decriminalization Policies in Practice around the Globe*, Release (2012). The latter summarizes some of the available research on decriminalization and demonstrates that the law enforcement model adopted has little impact on drug-prevalence rates within a given society. For more on why legalization will not turn us into a nation of addicts, see Steven B. Duke, *Drug Prohibition: An Unnatural Disaster*, Faculty Scholarship Series, paper 812 (1995) pp. 598-611. See also *supra* notes 71, 77, and *infra* notes 79, 82.

[80] Instead of addressing the underlying problems of drug use, prohibition has worsened the situation for drug users. As noted by Mike Trace, the former deputy UK Drug Czar: "Whereas much of the work of social affairs and development agencies at the national and international level have focused on improving the living conditions of poor and marginalised groups, and on promoting their social and economical integration in society, many aspects of drug control policies have had the opposite effect. Programmes focusing on widespread arrests and harsh sanctions towards drug users have lead to further marginalisation and stigmatisation, pushing them away from jobs, education and other health and social services, and driving them into more risky behaviours. This process of criminalisation and marginalisation is acknowledged by the United Nations as a major barrier to the global challenges of tackling HIV/AIDS, and of promoting social and economic development." Mike Trace, *Drug Policy: Lessons Learnt, and Options for the Future*, Global Commission on Drug Policies (2011), pp. 7-8.

This, again, is uncontroversial. For example, the authors of *Informing America's Policy on Illegal Drugs: What We Don't Know Keeps Hurting Us,* National Research Council (2001), point out that many of the harms associated with drug use are caused or augmented by prohibition. In his *Drug Prohibition: A Legal and Economic Analysis,* professor Walter Block argues that present drug policies have increased crime, decreased respect for legitimate law, and created great social upheaval; the same conclusion is drawn by most of the reports and law reviews mentioned elsewhere, and Professor Andrew Koppelman speaks to it thus: "It is true that many drug abusers in contemporary America are in wretched health, undernourished and sickly, and that many of them are infected with AIDS, often as a result of shared needles for intravenous drug use. Many steal to support their habits, and of course the drug trade produces enormous violence and corruption. These are, however, artifacts of illegality. If drugs were legal and cheap, these people would be able to get their supply with no danger to their health, and needle sharing would disappear. Drug addicts could live more comfortably than they do now." Andrew Koppelman, *Drug Policy and the Liberal Self* (2006), p. 286, sources omitted.

Another scholar, Doug Bandow, elaborates: "Prohibition is advanced as a means to protect users from themselves. . . . However, the illegal marketplace makes drug use more dangerous. Noted economists Daniel K. Benjamin and Roger Leroy Miller, "Many of the most visible adverse effects attributed to drug use . . . are due not to drug use per se, but to our current public policy toward drugs". Products are adulterated; users have no means of guaranteeing quality. Given the threat of discovery, dealers prefer to transport and market more potent (and thus both more concealable and valuable) drugs. As a result, the vast majority of "drug-related" deaths are "drug law-related" deaths." Doug Bandow, *From Fighting the Drug War to Protecting the Right to Use Drugs: Recognizing a Forgotten Liberty* (2012), p. 268.

To put the damages caused by prohibition in perspective, drug analyst James Ostrowski estimates that 80% of the world's 160,000 drug-use-deaths are caused by prohibition, while only 20% by the inherent qualities of the drugs (Ostrowski, *The Moral and Practical Case for Drug Legalization*, p. 654). As he explains: "A given amount of legal drug use would cause much less death and illness than the same quantity of illegal drug use. A realistic estimate is that illegal drug use is five times more dangerous than legal use. This means that even a highly unlikely five-fold increase in drug use under legalization would not increase the current number of drug overdose deaths. That is: the yearly number of heroin and cocaine deaths combined is about 3,000 per year. Of the 3,000 deaths, 80 percent or 2,400 deaths are caused by black market factors, while 20 percent or 600 deaths are caused by the intrinsic effects of the drugs. Thus, if under legalization legal drug use remained at the same level as current illegal use, there would be only 600 deaths each year. Only a five-fold or 500 percent increase in use would match the current black market death toll. Furthermore, it would take a 1,200 percent increase in legal drug use to produce as many deaths as prohibition causes through murder, AIDS, and poisoned drugs. Prohibition now causes 7,925 deaths, while 600 are the result of the drugs themselves. Thus, in order for legalized drug use to match the overall death toll of prohibition, use would have to increase more than thirteen-fold." Ostrowski, *The Moral and Practical Case for Drug Legalization*, Hofstra Law Review: Vol. 18:607 (1990), p. 669-70 (sources omitted).

The same argument, that "even if consumption of legalized drugs increased tenfold under a repeal regime, the physical harms associated with drug use could be less than under prohibition," is presented by Steven B. Duke in *Drug Prohibition: An Unnatural Disaster*, p. 600. That said, no serious scholar expects such an increase in drug use. In fact, even a 100 percent increase is highly unlikely, as there is evidence that prohibition has had little effect on drug use rates.

For more on the harms caused drug users by criminalization, see The Alternative World Drug Report: *Counting the Costs of the War on Drugs* (2012) pp. 61-97; Warren Redlich, *A Substantive Due Process Challenge to the War on Drugs* p. 15-20; INPUD, *Drug User Peace Initiative: Stigmatising People who Use Drugs* (2014); and Rodrigo Uprimny, Diana Guzman and Jorge Parra, *Addicted to Punishment: The Disproportionality of Drug Laws in Latin America* (2012). See also *supra* notes 45, 71, 77, and *infra* note 82.

[81] Every honest student of drug policy will conclude that the harms caused by prohibition transcend the harms caused by the drugs. See, for instance, Andrew Koppelman, *Drug Policy and the Liberal Self*, p.286; Warren Redlich, *A Substantive Due Process Challenge to the War on Drugs*, pp. 15-16; Ernest Drucker, *Drug prohibition and public health: 25 years of evidence*, Public Health Reports, (January 1, 1999); James Ostrowski, *Thinking about Drug Legalization*, Policy Analysis No. 121, Cato Institute (1989) at notes 47-51 and accompanying text; Daniel Polsby, *Legalization Is the Prudent Thing to Do*, in Timothy Lynch (ed.), *After Prohibition: an Adult Approach to Drug Policies in the 21st Century*, The Cato Institute (2000). As professor Polsby therein states: "Without in any way minimizing

the social costs that would undoubtedly flow from legalizing drugs, it is simply incredible to believe that the costs of pursuing the policy of minimizing drug use through the criminal law has not been many, many times more expensive, in treasure, shattered lives, and nasty externalities that have been borne by virtually the entire country."(p. 174.)

We have already presented some of the evidence. However, the damage done to drug users is not the whole story. Professor of law Randy Barnett elaborates: "When I was a prosecutor, over half of the murders I prosecuted were "drug law related" in the sense that the victim was killed as a result of a drug deal gone bad or a robbery of someone suspected of having either valuable drugs or money from selling drugs."(Barnett, *Bad Trip: Drug Prohibition and the Weakness of Public Policy,* p. 4.) This figure is supported by research mentioned by Ostrowski in *The Moral and Practical Case for Drug Legalization* (pp. 648-50), where he concludes that some 40 percent of US murders are drug-law related. Professor Steven Duke elaborates on similar findings: "In many cities, such as New Haven, Connecticut, at least half of the killings are drug-business related. Nationwide, between 5,000 and 10,000 murders per year are systemic to the drug business. Thus, more people are killed by the prohibition of drugs than by the drugs themselves." Steven B. Duke, *Drug Prohibition: An Unnatural Disaster,* Faculty Scholarship Series, paper 812 (1995) p. 577, sources omitted.

Furthermore, in Latin America, the Grupo de Apoyo Mutuo Foundation in Guatemala estimates that 45 percent of all homicides in that country are drug trafficking related. (Organization of American States, *The Drug Problem in the Americas* (2013), p. 76) Other countries in the region are not better off. As mentioned, it is estimated that 150,000 murders in the Americas are drug war related and that prohibition kills many more than the drugs themselves. As stated by the OAS: "By any standard of comparison, the number of deaths caused by drug use appears minimal when compared with the deaths from criminal actions related to drug trafficking. The government of Mexico estimated that between December 2006 and January 2012, approximately 60,000 people died in that country as a result of executions, clashes between rival groups, and attacks on the authorities by criminal organizations involved in drug trafficking. During that same period, the World Health Organization (WHO) recorded 563 deaths in Mexico from overdoses of controlled drugs." Organization of American States, *The Drug Problem in the Americas* (2013), p. 84.

As a matter of fact, the more repressive the law-and-order approach, the more likely it is to foster crime than public safety. This point is no longer controversial. After reviewing all available English language peer-reviewed research on the impact of prohibition on drug market violence, researchers Dan Werb, Greg Rowell, Gordon Guyatt, Thomas Kerr, Julio Montaner and Evan Wood concluded: "The available scientific evidence suggests that increasing the intensity of law enforcement interventions to disrupt drug markets is unlikely to reduce drug gang violence. Instead, the existing evidence suggests that drug-related violence and high homicide rates are likely a natural consequence of drug prohibition. . . . In this context, and since drug prohibition has not achieved its stated goal of reducing drug supply, alternative models for drug control may need to be considered if drug supply and drug-related violence are to be meaningfully reduced." Werb et al., *Effect of Drug Law Enforcement on Drug-Related Violence: Evidence from a Scientific Review*, International Centre for Science in Drug Policy (2010), p. 5-6.

This is why knowledgeable scholars are certain that a regulation of drugs is the only way to go. For a more elaborate account of the harms caused by prohibition, see The Alternative World Drug Report: *Counting the Costs of the War on Drugs* (2012), pp.15-97; Jeffrey A. Miron, *A Critique of Estimates of the Economic Costs of Drug Abuse*, Drug Policy Alliance (2003), pp. 9-20; James Ostrowski, *The Moral and Practical Case for Drug Legalization*, Hofstra Law Review: Vol. 18:607 (1990), pp. 641-69; Steven B. Duke, *Mass Imprisonment, Crime Rates, and the Drug War: A Penological and Humanitarian Disgrace*, Faculty Scholarship Series Paper 826 (2010), pp. 4-6; Steven B. Duke, *Drug Prohibition: An Unnatural Disaster*, Faculty Scholarship Series, paper 812 (1995), pp. 575-98; Randy E. Barnett, *The Harmful Side Effects of Drug Prohibition*, Utah Law Review No. 1 (2009), pp. 11-34; *supra* note 79 and *infra* notes 82, 83, 84. For more on why law enforcement strategies tend to increase drug market-related violence, see the June 2011 report of the Global Commission on Drug

Policy, p.15; and McSweeney et al., *Tackling Drug Markets & Distribution Networks in the UK London*, UK Drug Policy Commission (2008).

[82] "The available evidence suggests that in the past two decades, US anti-drug policies—focused on prohibiting drug production, trade, and consumption, and punishing those involved—have done little to diminish the problems they were designed to address. They have neither curbed the supply nor reduced the consumption of illegal substances in the United States. In countries across the globe, drug-related problems, such as organized crime, violence, and corruption have worsened as a result. In some countries these issues threaten the political and social stability of the state." Peter Hakim, *Rethinking US Drug Policy*, Inter-American Dialogue/the Beckley Foundation (2011), p. 1. For more on drug prohibition being a threat to civilization, see WACD, *Not Just in Transit: Drugs, the State and Society in West Africa*, An Independent Report of the West Africa Commission on Drugs (June 2014); and Werb et al., *Effect of Drug Law Enforcement on Drug-Related Violence: Evidence from a Scientific Review*, International Centre for Science in Drug Policy (2010).

[83] Prohibitionists argue that there is a well-established relationship between drugs and crime. This, however, is wrong. For example, a study of crime and drug use among 9,945 Philadelphia men in their late twenties conducted in 1972 for the National Commission on Marijuana and Drug Abuse found that "available data did not permit a conclusion that drug use caused more crime or more serious crime." Laurent Laniel has more to say on this issue: "independent researchers say that the causal relationship between drugs and crime is merely a hypothesis that has not been proven true. Two scholars from the Earl Warren Legal Institute of the University of California at Berkeley, Franklin Zimring and Gordon Hawkins, who have published a highly regarded study of drug control problems in 1995, even contend that it is untrue. Indeed, they argue that while "it is beyond dispute that drug use and crime overlap and interact in a multiplicity of ways", the higher rate of drug use among offenders could be explained by factors in their personality, such as a higher propensity for taking risks and "a willingness to ignore the threat of moral condemnation", that lead them to both commit crimes and take drugs. In this view, both drugs and crime are simultaneous but

independent consequences of other variables; in simple terms: it is not drug use that causes crime but rather other factors that lead the vast majority of those who commit crime to also take drugs." Laurent Laniel, *The Relationship between Research and Drug Policy in the United States*, Management of Social Transformations, Discussion Paper No. 44, p.17, sources omitted.

Another scholar, Steven Duke, has this to say on the alleged link between drug use and crime: "Contrary to what our government told us when it imposed drug prohibition, most illegal recreational drugs have no pharmacological properties that produce violence or other criminal behavior. Heroin and marijuana diminish rather than increase aggressive behavior. Cocaine—or cocaine withdrawal—occasionally triggers violence but usually does not. Very little crime is generated by the mere use of these drugs, especially in comparison to alcohol, which is causally related to thousands of homicides and hundreds of thousands of assaults annually. The major linkages between illegal drugs and crime must be found elsewhere—in prohibition. . . . [In fact,] the drug war as it is currently being waged probably produces at least half of our serious crime. That is, half of our crime (not counting drug crimes, of course) simply would not occur were we not conducting a drug war. No more damning an indictment of our political leaders can be imagined than that they have affirmatively created half the crime under which we suffer." Steven B. Duke, *Drug Prohibition: An Unnatural Disaster*, Faculty Scholarship Series, paper 812 (1995) p. 575, 581, sources omitted.

While prohibitionists will disagree, the criminogenic effects of prohibition are undisputable. We have already seen (*supra* note 80) that hundreds of thousands of murders are the direct result of prohibition, but there is more. As Duke alludes to above, murder, kidnapping, and violence is only one aspect of the illegal economy, as prohibition also encourages crimes like theft and burglary. *In other words, prohibition, not drug use, generates crime.* This is further documented by researchers Katherine Beckett and Steve Herbert: "Contrary to what this theory would predict, the evidence suggests that drug arrests in general, and marijuana arrests in particular, do not lower criminal activity, and may actually increase crime. For example, researchers using Florida data found that every additional drug arrest led to an increase in 0.7 index crimes. That is, for every 10 additional drug arrests, there were an additional 7 index (violent and property) crimes. A similar but more recent study found that a 1% increase in drug arrests leads to a .18% increase in index crimes. And a study of New York state law enforcement practices reports that rising numbers of drug arrests resulted in a significant increase in assaults, robberies, burglaries, and larcenies. For example, the authors report that a 10% increase in marijuana sales arrests was accompanied by an additional 800 larcenies in the state. Collectively, these studies show that increased law enforcement attention to drug crimes is associated with higher rather than lower levels of serious crime. To explain these correlations, researchers theorize that shifting limited resources to drug law enforcement adversely affects law enforcement's ability to respond to, investigate, and solve crimes with victims, thus leading to an increase in the number of such crimes." Katherine Beckett and Steve Herbert, *The Consequences and Costs of Marijuana Prohibition* (2006), p. 31.

For an elaboration on how and why prohibition generates crime and other negative externalities, see Bruce L. Benson, *The War on Drugs: A Public Bad* (2008), pp. 4-36; James Ostrowski, *Answering the Critics of Drug Legalization* pp. 12-13; Rasmussen and Benson, *Rationalizing Drug Policy under Federalism*, pp. 685-711. For more on why prohibition is not justified to prevent crime, see DOUGLAS HUSAK, LEGALIZE THIS! THE CASE FOR DECRIMINALIZING DRUGS (Verso 2002), pp. 82-93; and JAMES B. BAKALAR & LESTER GRINSPOON, DRUG CONTROL IN A FREE SOCIETY, Cambridge University Press (1998), p. 133.

[84] For more on why prohibition is not justified to protect our children, see DOUGLAS HUSAK, LEGALIZE THIS! THE CASE FOR DECRIMINALIZING DRUGS (Verso 2002), pp. 67-82. See also Rolles et al., *After the War on Drugs: Options for Control*, Transform Drug Policy Foundation (2004), pp. 27.28.

[85] Prohibitionists argue that drug use would skyrocket if it were not for their law-and-order approach. This, however, is wrong, as researchers have shown "that regulating the cannabis market through law enforcement has only a marginal, if any, effect on the level of cannabis consumption." For more on this, see Dirk Korf, *An Open Front Door: The Coffee Shop*

*Phenomenon in the Netherlands*, in EMCDDA, *A Cannabis Reader: Global Issues and Local Experiences*, Monograph series 8, Volume 1 (2008); Reuband, *Drug use and drug policy in Western Europe: Epidemiological findings in a comparative perspective*, European Addiction Research 1 (1–2) (1995), pp. 32–41. For more on why drug use would not skyrocket, see Ostrowski, *The Moral and Practical Case for Drug Legalization* (1990), pp. 672-75; and MIKALSEN, *HUMAN RISING*, (2010) pp. 440-42. For case studies documenting that decriminalization have little or no effect on user prevalence, see the June 2011 report of the Global Commission on Drug Policy pp. 10-11; Katherine Beckett and Steve Herbert, *The Consequences and Costs of Marijuana Prohibition* (2006); and *A Wiser Path: Ending Prohibition*, The New York Bar Association (1994). For more on why legalization is a more humane approach, see Warren Redlich, *A Substantive Due Process Challenge to the War on Drugs*, pp. 17-20.

All summed up, if we exclude the war profiteers and gangsters, it is hard to see any way prohibition benefits society. Steven Duke speaks to it thus: "The costs of drug prohibition are undeniably huge. But what of the benefits? Sadly, there probably are none to the society at large. Drug dealers owe their livelihoods to prohibition, as do thousands of drug warriors. Prison builders benefit, as do politicians who owe their careers to their opposition to demon "drugs." Inner-city morticians who dress bodies of victims of drug war turf battles, car dealers and jewelers who sell their goods to drug distributors, and other satellite entrepreneurs benefit from drug prohibition, but only those who make money from the drug war benefit from it. Everyone else suffers greatly." Steven B Duke, *Drug Prohibition: An Unnatural Disaster*, p. 598.

[86] Many prohibitionists rely on studies of the economic and social costs of drug abuse to justify their policies. Despite the enormity of these estimates, however, such studies provide no evidence on the merits of prohibition. These studies document harms that occur under prohibition, but they contain no information on whether prohibition increases or decreases the harms from drug abuse. A valid analysis of prohibition, to quote Miron, "must specify an alternative policy, such as legalization, and compare prohibition to this alternative with respect to each of three issues: (1) The direct costs of

enforcing the policies; (2) The auxiliary consequences of the policies; and (3) The effects of the policies on the harms from drug use."

Such analysis is a difficult undertaking. Nevertheless, when the pros and cons are considered, it will not look good for the prohibitionists. I only know of two studies which have attempted this task. One is Rolles (ed.), *A Comparison of the Cost-effectiveness of Prohibition and Regulation of Drugs*, Transform Drug Policy Foundation (April 2009). The other is James Ostrowski, *The Moral and Practical Case for Drug Legalization*, where Ostrowski concludes that 80 percent of all the economic and social costs of drug abuse are attributable to prohibition (p. 662).

For more on what issues a scientific evaluation must address and why the costs of drug abuse do not legitimize a prohibition, see Jeffrey A. Miron, *A Critique of Estimates of the Economic Costs of Drug Abuse*, Drug Policy Alliance (2003).

[87] To understand why the moral argument fails, see HUSAK, *LEGALIZE THIS! THE CASE FOR DECRIMINALIZING DRUGS* (Verso 2002), pp. 109-124; DAVID A. J. RICHARDS, *SEX, DRUGS, DEATH AND THE LAW: AN ESSAY ON HUMAN RIGHTS AND OVERCRIMINALIZATION* (Rowman & Littlefield 1986), pp. 168-85; Doug Bandow, *From Fighting the Drug War to Protecting the Right to Use Drugs: Recognizing a Forgotten* Liberty, in Fred McMahon (ed.), Towards a Worldwide Index of Human Freedom, Fraser Institute (2012), p. 259-64; and Nilsen & Blumenson, *Liberty Lost: the Moral Case for Marijuana Law Reform*, pp. 6-11.

[88] For a critique of such paternalistic arguments, see Nilsen & Blumenson, *Liberty Lost: The Moral Case for Marijuana Law Reform*, p. 11-19; Doug Bandow, *From Fighting the Drug War to Protecting the Right to Use Drugs: Recognizing a Forgotten Liberty*, pp. 258-59; Ostrowski, *The Moral and Practical Case for Drug Legalization*, pp. 632-35; HUSAK, *LEGALIZE THIS! THE CASE FOR DECRIMINALIZING DRUGS* (Verso 2002), pp. 93-108; HUSAK, *DRUGS AND RIGHTS* (Cambridge University Press 1996), pp. 71-144.

[89] Marijuana is no more a gateway to harder drugs than milk, coffee, beer, or cigarettes. Numerous studies have confirmed this, including a study funded by the National Institute of Medicine at the instigation of former Drug Czar

Barry McCaffrey (Janet E. Joy, Stanley J. Watson, Jr., and John A. Benson, Jr., *Marijuana and Medicine: Assessing the Science Base*). This study found no causal relationship between marijuana use and use of hard drugs. This should come as no surprise, as there is nothing in marijuana that makes the user crave or desire drugs like heroin or cocaine. For more on this, see Erich Goode, *Drugs in American Society* (1993), pp. 203-07; House of Commons Science and Technology Committee, *Drug classification: making a hash of it?* Fifth Report of Session (2005–06), p. 25-26; Jacob Sullum, *Saying Yes: In Defense of Drug Use* (Tarcher/Penguin, 2004), pp.126-30.

[90] For more on this, see Doug Bandow, *From Fighting the Drug War to Protecting the Right to Use Drugs: Recognizing a Forgotten Liberty*, pp. 256-58. He explains: "The criminal law normally applies to direct rather than indirect harm, that is, when individual rights (to be secure in one's person or property, for instance) are violated. The criminal must cause the harm to others, rather than engage in otherwise legal conduct which causes incidental loss. Moreover, only some drug use some of the time hurts others. Observed Robert J. MacCoun of the University of California (Berkeley) and Peter Reuter of the University of Maryland, "it is likely that many if not most drug users never do wrongful harm to others as a result of their using careers." (p.257, sources omitted)

Further elaboration is provided in James Ostrowski, *Answering the Critics of Drug Legalization*. As he makes clear: "[Prohibitionists] make the irresistible argument that drug use is not a "victimless crime". But this is sheer word play. Such an argument involves changing the definition of "victim" without telling the audience. Drug use certainly is a victimless crime if victim is defined in the traditional sense as one who has been subjected to force or fraud by a criminal. Drug offenses are also victimless crimes because one can be convicted of violating them even though no actual harm has been done to anyone. [Prohibitionists], however, uses the term victimless crime in a totally different sense. Drug use is a "victimful" crime because some of the people who use drugs do bad things to others allegedly because of their drug-taking. There are numerous problems with this argument. First, it assumes that drug use, as opposed to personality and other factors, is a major cause of harmful conduct. However, it is very difficult to prove this causal relationship. Nevertheless, under legalization, any actual harm a drug user might cause to person or property would be punishable and/or compensable under existing law. Furthermore, greater resources would be available to deal with actual third-party harm from drug use once these resources were no longer devoted to preventing and punishing drug use per se. This solution to the problem is far better than punishing all drug users to prevent some from possibly harming others. The rights of all drug users should not be infringed solely because prohibition might prevent some drug users from causing harm to third parties, when such harm is already unlawful. Besides, outlawing drug use because some users might harm others is self-contradictory since it necessitates harming many drug users who themselves have harmed no one. Finally, any third-party harm caused by illegal drug use today is dwarfed by the third-party harm caused by illegal drug laws. Ironically, while drug users under legalization would be legally responsible for the harm they cause to third parties, prohibitionists today are not at all responsible for the harm they cause to others. Thus, the moral argument from third-party consequences actually runs in favor of legalization, not against." James Ostrowski, *Answering the Critics of Drug Legalization*, 5 Notre Dame J.L. Ethics & Pub. Policy 823 (1991), pp. 835-36, sources omitted. For a fuller elaboration on why prohibition cannot be justified on the grounds that drug use harms others, see Douglas Husak, *Drugs and Rights* (Cambridge University Press 1996), pp. 145-208.

[91] Prohibitionists, when all else fails, have tried to argue that any uncertainty favors the status quo. This is false, as they cannot legitimize a state of eternal war on the grounds that we do not know the consequences of peace. To the contrary, the law is clear: We begin with a presumption of liberty and any doubt favors the legalization argument. In *the Moral and Practical Case for Drug Legalization*, Ostrowski not only discusses the burden of proof, but elaborates on the implications. For prohibition to continue, he argues that "supporters of prohibition must demonstrate all of the following: (1) the use of currently illegal drugs is immoral; (2) the state has the right to enforce this moral rule; (3) the state can effectively enforce this moral rule without creating additional problems as serious as drug use itself; that is: (a) that

drug use would increase substantially after legalization; (b) that the harm caused by any increased drug use would not be offset by the increased safety of legal drug use; (c) that the harm caused by any increased use would not be offset by a reduction in the use of dangerous drugs that are already legal (e.g., alcohol and tobacco); and (d) that the harm caused by any increased drug use not offset by (b) or (c) would exceed the  harm now caused by the side effects of prohibition (e.g., crime and corruption). In the absence of data supporting these propositions, neither the theoretical danger of illegal drugs nor their actual harmful effects, are a sufficient basis for prohibition. Even if it were proven that drug use would rise if legalized, such proof would be insufficient to support prohibition. Prohibitionists face a daunting task—one that no one has yet accomplished or, apparently, even attempted."

The case for legalization, on the other hand, "is sustained if any of the following propositions is true: (1) regardless of whether the use of currently illegal drugs is immoral, the state has no moral right to enforce this moral prohibition because doing so would violate individual rights; (2) prohibition has no  substantial impact on the level of illegal drug use; (3) prohibition increases illegal drug use; (4) prohibition merely redistributes drug use from illegal drugs to harmful legal drugs; (5) even though prohibition might decrease the use of illegal drugs, the negative effects of prohibition outweigh the beneficial effects of reduced illegal drug use." James Ostrowski, *The Moral and Practical Case for Drug Legalization*, Hofstra Law Review: Vol. 18:607 (1990), pp. 616-17 (sources omitted).

[92] In its General Comment 31, paragraph 16, the Human Rights Committee elaborates: "Article 2, paragraph 3, requires that States Parties make reparation to individuals whose Covenant rights have been violated. Without reparation to individuals whose Covenant rights have been violated, the obligation to provide an effective remedy, which is central to the efficacy of article 2, paragraph 3, is not discharged. In addition to the explicit reparation required by articles 9, paragraph 5, and 14, paragraph 6, the Committee considers that the Covenant generally entails appropriate compensation. The Committee notes that, where appropriate, reparation can involve restitution, rehabilitation and measures of satisfaction, such as public apologies, public memorials, guarantees of non-repetition and changes in relevant laws and

practices, as well as bringing to justice the perpetrators of human rights violations".

[93] General Comment no. 31, paragraph 18.